By

نيرمين عبد العزيز حمودة

Nermein Abdul-Azeez Hammouda

Know Arabic Productions

www.knowarabic.co.uk

Acknowledgements

I would like to thank the Adult Education service in England for the Arabic language courses they have made available in Coventry and Leamington, and for all my students whose presence made this book come to light. I would also like to thank the Authors of all the work that has set a good foundation for teaching this beautiful language to non-Arabic speakers. I also thank my children who have been my students and helped me with the book and game creation.

Dedication

I would like to dedicate this book firstly to my Mentor, and to all the Arabic language teachers who have taught me the beauty and uniqueness of this language since childhood. Especially to Dr. Ahmad AlKobeisy, Dr. Fadel Assamerra'i and Dr. Yossry Gabr for being an inspiration to me through their knowledge which they have made available for everyone around the world.

إِلى روحِ خَيْرِ مَنْ تَكَلَّمَ بِالعَرَبِيَّة

Contents

Part 1

Introduction

Learning a new language is an exciting journey that opens new worlds. Many people think of Arabic as an entirely foreign language, yet it shares some very interesting linguistic roots with other Western Languages, along with significant historical interactions. The Arabic vocabulary that exists in the English language today is a witness to these shared roots.

I am very passionate about teaching the Arabic Language, Culture and History. And throughout my years of experience in teaching, I realised that there is a strong need to do more to share the great benefits this language has to offer. I also found that learners may find it confusing to choose between Classical Arabic, also called Modern Standard Arabic - MSA, and Colloquial Arabic.

The approach I took in this book is to teach Classical Arabic and the Colloquial form closest to it, I explain how to derive the colloquial form in simple steps. In this way, you will have a sound linguistic base which is used in Formal settings and in the Arabic Media and literature, and you will also be able to live and communicate comfortably in any Arab country.

Hope you enjoy the book.

Nermein Hammouda

08/02/2019

England

Introduction to Arabic

What is Arabic?

The beauty of learning a language such as Arabic, is that it looks and sounds completely different. People often find its sound very enchanting, especially in the Classical form. This is besides its beautiful Calligraphy which is also used as a form of Art on its own.

Arabic is an old Semitic Language spoken originally in the Arabic Peninsula. And now it is the mother tongue of nations living in the Middle East and North Africa. Semitic languages are a Group of Ancient Languages that originated mainly from the Middle East, and they include Aramaic, Hebrew, Phoenician, Syriac and Ugaritic.

It is said that the first speaker of Arabic was Ismael, son of Abraham and Hagar. He was born around 4000 years ago in Mecca. He is the son of Abraham who is considered the Father of Abrahamic Religions, and an Egyptian mother called Hagar, a highly regarded mother figure in Arabic history. And hence, he is the son of two Great Civilisations: Egypt and Mesopotamia.

There are many Arabic words that exist in the English language today, like: Algebra, Alcohol Algorithms, Banana, Chemistry, Coffee, Jar, Sofa, Sugar, Tariff, etc. These words transferred mainly through the influence of Al-Andalus in the Middle Ages, the renowned advanced Civilization which lasted around eight centuries, and provided a strong base of our modern-day Civilization.

Why Learn Arabic?

Arabic is the official language of 26 Countries. The fifth most spoken in the world, and one of the languages of the United Nations. It is the mother tongue of over 400 million people living in the Arab world and the Religious Language of over 2 billion Muslims who read the Quran; the most authentic Arabic text that reached us unchanged since the 6th Century and is wholly memorised by millions of people.

Arabic is an excellent language to learn for a variety of reasons:

Tourism:

- The Arab World is an ancient region that is very rich in history and monuments.
- It has some of the world's best resorts which lie on different seas, rivers, greeneries, deserts, and mountains.
- Arabs are known to be a friendly and hospitable nation who have a lot of heritage to introduce to the world.

Business:

- The Arab World is a rapidly growing region and is full of business opportunities that attract many investors and expatriates who learn the language to interact with people and have more comfort living in an Arab country.

Religious / Spiritual reasons:

- Quran Recitation:

  Muslims believe that the Quran is a holy book that descended through Prophet Mohammad. The Arabic language is considered a great carrier for this message through its special characteristics, therefore, understanding it directly is very important as part of religious activities. Quran recitation is also used for spiritual healing through the strong positive vibes of its sound.

The Arabic Language special character

Root and Branches

Most Arabic words are built on a Root of Three letters, and from this root stems a Group of words with shared meanings. This feature is very helpful for a deeper and broader understanding of meanings.

Examples:

See the different words that stem from the same Three letters Root, and they are all related:

- TO WRITE   كَ تَ بَ

مَكْتَب (Office) - مَكْتَبَة (Library) - كِتاب (Book) - كاتِب (Writer)

- TO FLY   طَ يَ رَ

طائِرَة (Airplane) - مَطار (Airport) - طائِر (Bird)

As you notice, different words are derived from the same root, and hence, links can be formed between them. Also, remembering these words becomes easier.

This Criteria of how words are built serves perfectly for a comprehensive understanding of Religious Laws and linking them to Spiritual concepts. To give you an example of this, look at the use of the words Islam and Share'a (Islamic law):

- Islam

  - **From the Root** م ل س

Words stemming from the Root م ل س :

Peace	سَلام
Submission	تَسْليم
Sound/ whole	سَليم
Safety	سَلامَة

Now you can create links between these words, and then you can understand the complete meaning of the word Islam.

- ## Share'a (Islamic Law)

  - **From the Root** ش ر ع

Words stemming from the Root ش ر ع :

Legislation	شَرْع
Road	شارِع
Sail	شِراع
Method	شِرْعَة
Project	مَشْروع
Place of water	مَشْرَعَة

Now you can now create a Two-Dimensional picture to understand the meaning of Share'a: It is a law, method, or project that you use as a sale for safety and nourishment (the source of water).

Having words sharing the exact same root or having the same root letters but in a different order also works well when understanding concepts through contradictions.

Examples:

  - **Root** ع ذ ب

<u>**Words stemming from the root عذب :**</u>

Anguish   عَذاب

Sweetness – Purity   عُذوبَة

This may indicate that trouble can also have a purifying effect and that it is also important to realize the sweet state of ease.

- <u>**The letters ن ح م in different orders:**</u>

Produce the Word مِحْنَة which means Distress. And the same letters in a different order produce the Word مِنْحَة which means Grant. This indicates that tough times could also be looked at as a gift for their possible positive effect.

The Arab World Map

The Arab Word consists of 22 countries. Located in Western Asia, North Africa, the Horn of Africa, and the Comoros Islands off the Cost of East Africa. The Region extends from the Atlantic Ocean in the West to the Arabian Sea in the East. And from the Mediterranean Ocean in the North to the Indian Ocean in the Southeast.

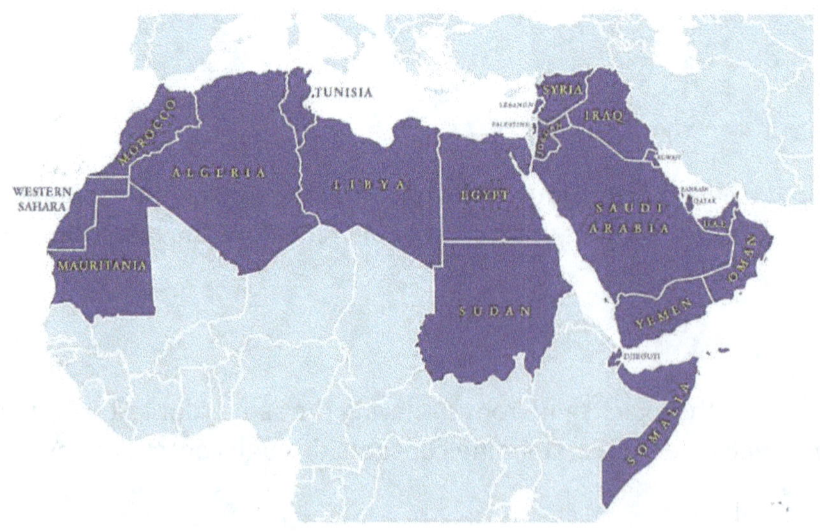

Countries are divided into Three main Regions according to their geographical position, common history, similar dialect, and culture:

Gulf Countries		The Levant		North Africa	
Saudi Arabia	السُّعودِيَّة	Syria	سوْريا	Egypt	مِصْر
Iraq	العِراق	Lebanon	لِبْنان	Sudan	السّودان
Kuwait	الكُوَيت	Palestine	فَلَسْطين	Djibouti	جيبوتي
Bahrain	البَحْرين	Jordan	الأُرْدُن	Somalia	الصّومال
Qatar	قَطَر			Comoros Islands	جُزُرُ القَمَر
United Arab Emirates	الإمارات			Libya	ليبْيا
Oman	عُمان			Tunisia	تونِس
Yemen	اليَمَن			Algeria	الجَزائِر
				Morocco	المَغْرِب
				Mauritania	موريتانْيا

Chapter One
The Arabic Alphabet: Consonants and Vowels

The Alphabet roots

Arabic Alphabet developed from Pictorial Symbols thousands of years ago in the Middle East. These are Protosemitic letters that connect sounds and meanings to symbols in nature. Interestingly, there are links between these symbols and the Latin Alphabet that exist today.

This table shows the evolving of Arabic letters from their symbolic roots, and you can also see the corresponding English letters. The proto-Semitic symbols come from basic life pictures. For example: the A أ is an Ox head, B ب is a house, R ر is a man's head , N ن is a sprout which means life, M م from water which means abundance , etc.

The following comparative table lists several ancient scripts (Caractères hiératiques égyptiens, Phéniciens, Hébraïque, Syriaque, Samaritain, Arabe) shown as glyphs, together with their value in French characters ("Valeur en caractères français"). The script-glyph columns contain handwritten characters; the readable French-value columns are transcribed below.

	Valeur en caractères français (Syriaque)		Valeur en caractères français (Samaritain)		Valeur en caractères français (Arabe)		Valeur en caractères français (Arabe suite)
	A		H		A		L
	B		S		B		M
	C		V		T		N
	D		H		Ts		U
	E		D		Dj		V
	F		G		H		Y
	Z		B		Kh		
	H		A		D		
	Th (@ grec)		E		Dz		
	I		Ç		R		
	K		N		Z		
	L		M		Sç		
	M		L		Chsch		
	N		K		Sc		
	Cs (= grec)		I		Dh		
	O		T		Th		
	P		Th		Dh		
	Ts		Sch		H		
	Q		R		G		
	R		Q		F		
	S		Tz		K		
	T		P		Oc		

The Arabic Alphabet

In Arabic we write from right to left. There are 28 letters in the Arabic language, some look identical except for the dots. When writing, most Arabic letters join to each other, and their shapes slightly differ depending on their position in the word.

In this book, the 28 Arabic letters will be divided into Six Groups. This is to slowly study how they are written at the start, middle, and end of a word. The division is based on the similarity of the letters' shapes and joining method.

الأَبْجَدِيَّةُ العَرَبِيَّة

The Arabic Alphabet

ث	ت	ب	أ
د	خ	ح	ج
س	ز	ر	ذ
ط	ض	ص	ش
ف	غ	ع	ظ
م	ل	ك	ق
ي	و	ه	ن

The Arabic Alphabet الحُروفُ الأَبْجَدِيَّةُ العَرَبِيَّة

أ Alef — A	ب Baa — B	ت Taa — T	ث Thaa — Th (Think)
ج Jeem — J	ح 7aa — 7	خ Khaa — Kh	
د Dal — D	ذ Thal — Th (The)	ر Raa — R	ز Zay — Z
س Seen — S	ش Sheen — Sh	ص Šaad — Š	ض Dhaad — Dh
ط Ṭa — Ṭ	ظ Ṭhaa — Ṭh	ع 3ein — 3	غ Ghein — Gh
ف Faa — F	ق Qaaf — Q	ك Kaaf — K	ل Laam — L
م Meem — M	ن Noon — N	ه Haa — H	و Waw — W
ي Yaa — Y			

Important Notes:

Some letters do not exist in English, other symbols may be used in this book to refer to them. These letters are:

The letter ح

ح The closest consonant to it is H. ح is pronounced from a deeper point of the throat. It can be referred to as a **H** or by using number **7**.

The letter خ

خ Is pronounced from the palate area. The letter exists in the German language, like the word Nacht. Interestingly, some English words still have an indication of the letter خ from its German root, like light and night. The letter faded away by time until it dissolved. It can be referred to as **Kh**.

The letter ص

ص Is a heavier form of س (S). It is referred to as **Š** in the previous table.

The letter ض

ض Is a heavier form of د (D). It can be referred to as **Dh**.

The letter ط

ط Is a heavier form of ت (T). It is referred to as **Ṭ** in the previous table.

The letter ظ

ظ Is a heavier form of ذ (Th). It is referred to as **Ťh** in the previous table.

The letter ع

ع Is pronounced from a deeper point of the throat The closest consonant to it is A. It can be referred to using number **3**.

The letter غ

غ Is pronounced from the Palate area and it is like the French pronunciation of R. It can be referred to as **Gh**.

The letter ق

ق Is a heavier form of ك (K). It can be referred to as **Q.**

Vowels

There are two types of Vowels in the Arabic Language. **Short Vowels** and **Long Vowels**.

Short vowels are separate symbols written on top of letters or below it, while **Long Vowels** are separate letters used as vowels (ي - و - ا), they are used to prolong a consonant just like in English.

- A consonant with a short vowel takes one tick of time (can be counted as one thumb movement)
- A Consonant followed by a long vowel is prolonged by two ticks.

Short vowels (Al-Harakat الحَرَكات)

There are mainly **Three Short Vowels** in Arabic. In addition to these, there is also a Pause and a Stress. These three short Vowels last for one tick of time which can be counted using one thumb movement.

These are the three main short Vowels:

1. **Fat7a (a)** فَتْحَة َ : A dash written **on top of a letter** as the mouth opens such as pronouncing the letter A:

بَ = Ba

2. **Dhamma (o)** ضَمَّة ُ : A small و Written **on top of a letter** as the mouth creates a circle shape such as pronouncing the letter O:

بُ = Bo

3. **Kasra (e)** كَسْرَة ِ : A dash Written **below the letter** as the mouth moves down such as pronouncing the letter E:

بِ = Be

In addition to these main three short Vowels there are other types of Vowels:

4. **<u>Sokoon</u> (Pause)** سُكون ْ : A circle written on top of the letter, and it indicates a Pause. This is a letter with no vowels.

بْ = B

5. <u>**Shadda**</u> (stress) شَدَّة ّْ◌ : Is written on top of the letter and it looks like the start of the letter س . It means that there are two letters together (as in the English language). In Arabic we write it as a stress sign, and it must have either *Fat7a* ◌َ, *Dhamma* ◌ُ or *Kasra* ◌ِ :

بَّ = Bba

بُّ = Bbo

بِّ = Bbe

6. **Tanween** تَنْوِين : Two short vowels of the same kind written together, and always occurring **at the end** of the word. We have three types of *Tanween*:

- **Tanween with Fat7 (تَنْوِين بِالفَتْح) .** ◌ً

  The letter is pronounced with *Fat7a* ◌َ + the letter *Noon* ن (N)
  (It is pronounced at the end of the word but not written).

  An Alef must be added - **in writing only** - to the letter that has *Tanween belFat7* at the end of the word. This applies for all letters except for the letters *Alef* أ and *Taa Marboota* ة (see notes about the letter ت in Letters Group 2) Which don't need an added *Alef* أ :

بًا = Ban

أً = An

ةً = Tan

- **Tanween with Dhamm (تَنْوين بالضَّم)** ٌ.

   The letter is pronounced with *Dhamma* ُ + the letter *Noon* ن (N)

   (It is pronounced at the end of the word but not written).

$$ بٌ = Bon $$

$$ أٌ = On $$

$$ ةٌ = Ton $$

- **Tanween with Kasr (تَنْوين بالكَسر)** ٍ.

   The letter is pronounced with *Kasra* ٍ + the letter *Noon* ن (N)

   (It is pronounced at the end of the word but not written).

$$ بٍ = Ben $$

$$ إٍ = In $$

$$ ةٍ = Ten $$

Now practice the Alphabet with all possible short vowels. And before moving onto long Vowels, which are basically three letters: ا – و – ي , we will first practice short vowels by learning how to form simple words using consonants and short vowels. We will do this by dividing the letters into **6 Groups**.

Note: You will find Audio files for the Alphabet section and other parts of the book in our website: **www.knowarabic.co.uk**

What these letters have in common is that they join with the previous letter, but they don't join with the following letter (they join from the right side but not the left).

Remember that we write from right to left in Arabic.

End	Middle	Beginning	Letter	
أُ ءُ ؤُ ئُ	ـأ	أ	أ	A
ـد	ـد	د	د	D
ـذ	ـذ	ذ	ذ	Th (Like The)
ـر	ـر	ر	ر	R
ـز	ـز	ز	ز	Z
ـو	ـو	و	و	W

Practice

End	Middle	Beginning	Letter
-------------------------------	-------------------------------	-------------------------------	أ
-------------------------------	-------------------------------	-------------------------------	د
-------------------------------	-------------------------------	-------------------------------	ذ
-------------------------------	-------------------------------	-------------------------------	ر
-------------------------------	-------------------------------	-------------------------------	ز
-------------------------------	-------------------------------	-------------------------------	و

End	Middle	Beginning	Letter
-------------------------------	-------------------------------	-------------------------------	أ
-------------------------------	-------------------------------	-------------------------------	د
-------------------------------	-------------------------------	-------------------------------	ذ
-------------------------------	-------------------------------	-------------------------------	ر
-------------------------------	-------------------------------	-------------------------------	ز
-------------------------------	-------------------------------	-------------------------------	و

Useful words consisting of Group 1 letters:

Translation	Phonetics	Arabic
And	Wa	وَ
Or	Aw	أَ + وْ = أَوْ
Rice	Rozz	رُ + زّ = رُزّ
Flowers	Ward	وَ + رْ + د = وَرْد

The letter Alef is also called Hamza and it has different rules for writing.

The letter Alef writing rules:

Also called Hamza referring to this part ء to identify it from the long Vowel ا which doesn't have the Hamza ء.

These rules are a bit advanced, and you can review it later if you want.

When the Hamza ء / أ comes in the middle or at the end of a word, we need to look at the *Haraka* (Short Vowel) **of the Hamza**, **and** the *Haraka* of the letter **before it** and compare according to the Vowel strength. The *Harakat* (Short Vowels) vary in strength. This is the order of its strength from strongest to weakest:

1: Kasra ـِ   *2: Dhamma* ـُ   *3: Fat7a* ـَ   *4: Sokoon* ـْ

Important Note: Long Vowels are considered to have Sokoon ـْ , and the Consonant letter followed by a long vowel is considered to have a short vowel identical to the following long vowel. So, if the letter is followed by an ا it will have ـْ , and if it is followed by a و it will have a ـُ , and if followed by a ي it will have a ـِ .

The main rules are:

- If the Alef or the letter before it has *Kasra* ـِ we write the Hamza like this:

تائِب – ذِئْب – مِئَة

- If the strongest of the two Vowels is *Dhamma* ـُ we write the Hamza *on a waw* و like this:

مُؤْمِن – بُؤْس – لُؤْلُؤ – مَيْؤوس – مَسْؤول – كُؤوس

- If the strongest of the two Vowels is *Fat7a* َ we write the Hamza on an Alef أ like

  this: مَنْأَى – رَأْفَة – مَلَأٌ

Other rules:

- If the Hamza has *Fat7a* َ or *Sokoon* ْ and comes after a long Vowel ا it is written
  on the line like this: عَباءَة – قِراءَة – ماء

- If the Hamza has *Fat7a* َ or *Sokoon* ْ and comes after a long Vowel و it is written
  on the line like this: نُبوءَة – مُروءَة – سوء – وُضوء

- If the Hamza has *Fat7a* َ and comes after a long Vowel ي It is written like this:
  هَنيئَة – بيئَة

Exercise 1: Translate these short sentences and practice writing them.

Rice and flowers.

Flowers or rice.

This group of letters look alike when they are in the start or the middle of a word, and they are differentiated by their dots. They join with letters from both sides.

End	Middle	Beginning	Letter	
			ب	B
			ت	T
			ث	Th (Like Think)
			ن	N
			ي	Y

Practice

End	Middle	Beginning	Letter
----------------------------	----------------------------	----------------------------	ب
----------------------------	----------------------------	----------------------------	ت
----------------------------	----------------------------	----------------------------	ث
----------------------------	----------------------------	----------------------------	ن
----------------------------	----------------------------	----------------------------	ي

End	Middle	Beginning	Letter
----------------------------	----------------------------	----------------------------	ب
----------------------------	----------------------------	----------------------------	ت
----------------------------	----------------------------	----------------------------	ث
----------------------------	----------------------------	----------------------------	ن
----------------------------	----------------------------	----------------------------	ي

<u>Important Note: The letter *Taa* ت</u>

ت Comes in two Forms at the end of a word:

1. ت :   This is called *Taa Maftoo7a* تاء مَفْتوحَة (An open *Taa*).
2. ة :   This is called *Taa Marboota* تاء مَرْبوطَة (A tied *Taa*).

- This first form: ت

   Means that when a word ending with ت stands alone, or lies at the end of a sentence, it will be pronounced as a ت with *Sokoon* ْ (Pause). When the ت is followed by another word it will have any other vowel.

Examples:

صَوْت – بِنْت – بَيْت – مُدَرِّسات – حَلَوِيّات

- The second form: ة

   Means that when a word ending with ة stands alone, or lies at the end of a sentence, it will be pronounced as a letter *Haa* ه with a *Sokoon* ْ. Otherwise, when followed by words, it will have any other short vowels and will be pronounced as a *Taa* ت .

We can say that the Taa Marboota ة is like a Hybrid of ت and ه .

Note: The *Taa Marboota* ة is used to transfer Masculine Nouns into Feminine Nouns. Like:

مُعَلِّمَة – طالِبَة – جَميلَة – كَبيرَة

See the Masculine and Feminine section of the book.

Useful words consisting of Group 2 letters:

Translation	Phonetics	Arabic
Coffee beans	Bonn	بُ + نّ = بُنّ
Girl	Bent	بِ + نْ + ت = بِنْت
House	Bayt-Clss/*Bate-Clq*	بَ + يْ + ت = بَيْت
Between	Bayna-Clss/*Bane-Clq*	بَ + يْ + ن = بَيْنَ

Note: Clss = Classical. *Clq = Colloquial.*

Useful words consisting of Group 1 and 2 letters:

Translation	Phonetics	Arabic
Father	Abb	أ + ب = أَب
Son	Ebn	إ + بْ + ن = إِبْن
Lord	Rabb	رَ + بّ = رَبّ
Land	Barr	بَ + رّ = بَرّ
Cold	Bard	بَ + رْ + د = بَرْد

Exercise 2: Translate the following and practice writing it.

أَبٌ وَ إِبْنٌ وَ بِنْت.

Exercise 3: Write the Arabic words for these pictures:

These letters have similar shapes, and dots are used to differentiate between them. They join with letters from both the right and the left sides. All of these letters except for ج (Jeem) don't exist in English.

End	Middle	Beginning	Letter	
			ج	J
			ح	7
			خ	Kh
			ع	3
			غ	Gh

Practice

End	Middle	Beginning	Letter
----------------------	----------------------	----------------------	ح
----------------------	----------------------	----------------------	ح
----------------------	----------------------	----------------------	خ
----------------------	----------------------	----------------------	ع
----------------------	----------------------	----------------------	غ

End	Middle	Beginning	Letter
----------------------	----------------------	----------------------	ح
----------------------	----------------------	----------------------	ح
----------------------	----------------------	----------------------	خ
----------------------	----------------------	----------------------	ع
----------------------	----------------------	----------------------	غ

Useful words consisting of Groups 1, 2 and 3 letters:

Translation	Phonetics	Arabic
Brother	Akh	أَ + خْ = أَخْ
Sister	Okht	أُ + خْ + تْ = أُخْت
Sea	Ba7r	بَ + خْ + ر = بَحْر
Grandfather	Jadd	جَ + دّ = جَدّ
Grandmother	Jaddah	جَ + دّ + ة = جَدَّة
Pocket	Jayb-Clss/*Jabe-Clq*	جَ + يْ + ب = جَيْب
Love	7obb	حُ + بّ = حُبّ
Pilgrimage	7ajj (Hajj)	حَ + جّ = حَجّ
Stone	7ajar	حَ + جَ + ر = حَجَر
Hot	7arr	حَ + رّ = حَرّ
Free (freedom)	7orr	حُ + رّ = حُرّ
Cheek	Khadd	خَ + دّ = خَدّ
Grapes	3enab	عِ + نَ + ب = عِنَب
Eye	3ayn-Clss/*3ane-Clq*	عَ + يْ + ن = عَيْن
Rich	Ghaneyy-Clss/*Ghani-Clq*	غَ + نِ + يّ = غَنِيّ

Exercise 4: Word Search puzzle.

Locate the words in the grids and cross them out, then form a word with the remaining letters (Letters can be used twice).

1:

Grapes – Love – Pocket – Hot – Rich – Sea – Free

ر	ح	ب	
	ب	ي	ج
ت		غ	أ
حَ	ب	ن	ع
زّ	حُ	ي	خ

The secret word is ………………………

2:

Flowers – Father – Grandfather – Hot – Stone – Girl – Eye – Sister

ن	ي	ع	ح	و
ب	أ	أ	ج	ر
ب	ت	خ	ر	د
ن		ت	ي	ح
ت	ب	د	ج	ر

The secret word is ………………………

Alphabet Group 4: س ش ص ض

These letters have similar shapes, and dots are used to differentiate between them. They join with letters from both the right and the left sides.

End	Middle	Beginning	Letter	
ـس	ـسـ	سـ	س	S
ـش	ـشـ	شـ	ش	Sh
ـص	ـصـ	صـ	ص	Š
ـض	ـضـ	ضـ	ض	Dh

Practice

End	Middle	Beginning	Letter
-------------------------	-------------------------	-------------------------	س
-------------------------	-------------------------	-------------------------	ش
-------------------------	-------------------------	-------------------------	ص
-------------------------	-------------------------	-------------------------	ض

End	Middle	Beginning	Letter
-------------------------	-------------------------	-------------------------	س
-------------------------	-------------------------	-------------------------	ش
-------------------------	-------------------------	-------------------------	ص
-------------------------	-------------------------	-------------------------	ض

Useful words consisting of Group 4 letters:

Translation	Phonetics	Arabic
Secret	Sirr	سِ + رّ = سِرّ
Evil	Sharr	شَ + رّ = شَرّ
Wellbeing /Good	Khayr-Clss/*Khare-Clq*	خَ + يْ + ر = خَيْر
Hunting /Fishing	Sayd-Clss/*Sade-Clq*	صَ + يْ + د = صَيْد
Harm	Dharar	ضَ + رَ + ر = ضَرَر

Exercise 5: Can you write these opposite words which you learned so far?

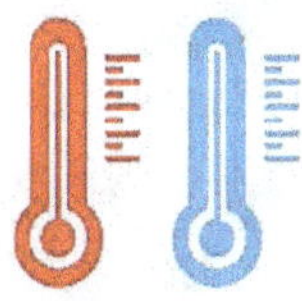

These letters join with letters from both the right and the left sides. The shapes of ط - ظ and ف - ق are similar, and the dots are used to differentiate between them.

End	Middle	Beginning	Letter	
ـط	ـطـ	طـ	ط	T
ـظ	ـظـ	ظـ	ظ	Heavy Th (Like Thus)
ـف	ـفـ	فـ	ف	F
ـق	ـقـ	قـ	ق	Q

Practice

End	Middle	Beginning	Letter
------------------------	------------------------	------------------------	ط
------------------------	------------------------	------------------------	ظ
------------------------	------------------------	------------------------	ف
------------------------	------------------------	------------------------	ق

End	Middle	Beginning	Letter
------------------------	------------------------	------------------------	ط
------------------------	------------------------	------------------------	ظ
------------------------	------------------------	------------------------	ف
------------------------	------------------------	------------------------	ق

Useful words consisting of Group 5 letters:

Translation	Phonetics	Arabic
Envelope	Tharf	ظَ + رْ + ف = ظَرْف
Guest	Dhayf-Clss/*Dafe-Clq*	ضَ + يْ + ف = ضَيْف
Time	Waqt	وَ + قْ + ت = وَقْت
Stop	Qef	قِ + فْ = قِفْ
Cat	Qett	قِ + طّ = قِطّ

Exercise 6: Write down the Arabic Words for these Pictures:

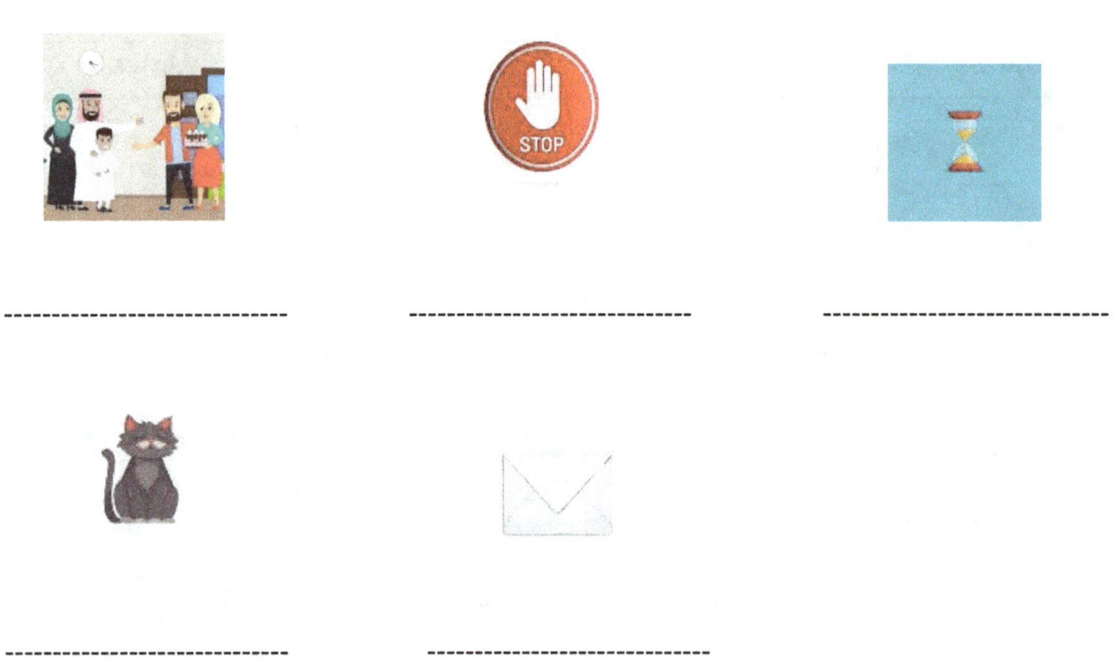

-----------------------------   -----------------------------   -----------------------------

-----------------------------   -----------------------------

Alphabet Group 6: ك ل م ه

These are the last 4 letters of the Alphabet. These letters join with letters from both the right and the left sides.

End	Middle	Beginning	Letter	
ـك	ـكـ	كـ	ك	K
ـل	ـلـ	لـ	ل	L
ـم	ـمـ	مـ	م	M
ـه	ـهـ	هـ	ه	H

Note: The letter ه looks like a circle if it is standing alone or if the preceding letter does not connect from the left side (Group 1 letters).

Practice

End	Middle	Beginning	Letter
-------------------------	-------------------------	-------------------------	ك
-------------------------	-------------------------	-------------------------	ل
-------------------------	-------------------------	-------------------------	م
-------------------------	-------------------------	-------------------------	ه

End	Middle	Beginning	Letter
-------------------------	-------------------------	-------------------------	ك
-------------------------	-------------------------	-------------------------	ل
-------------------------	-------------------------	-------------------------	م
-------------------------	-------------------------	-------------------------	ه

Useful words consisting of Group 6 letters:

Translation	Phonetics	Arabic
King	Malek	مَ + لِ + ك = مَلِك
Lock	Qefl	قِ + فْ + ل = قِفْل
Rope	7abl	حَ + بْ + ل = حَبْل
Dog	Kalb	كَ + لْ + ب = كَلْب

Exercise 7: Write the Arabic words under the pictures.

------------------   ------------------   ------------------   ------------------

------------------   ------------------   ------------------   ------------------

------------------   ------------------   ------------------   ------------------

Exercise 8: Join the letters to form words. Look up the meaning of new words.

أُ + مّ =	أَ + ب =
فَ + وْ + ق =	تَ + خْ + ت =
ظَ + رْ + ف =	بَ + يْ + ت =
أَ + خْ =	أُ + خْ + ت =
قَ + لَ + م =	لَ + وْ + ن =
هَ + رَ + م =	ضَ + يْ + ف =
بِ + نْ + ت =	وَ + لَ + د =
وَ + جْ + ه =	رَ + أْ + س =
قَ + مَ + ر =	شَ + مْ + س =

Exercise 9: Test yourself with these opposites which you have learned.

Hot and cold

Land and sea

Sun and Moon

Good and evil

Long Vowels   المَدّ

The second type of Vowels in Arabic are long Vowels. These take two Thumb movements (up=1, down=2). These Vowels are: ا – و – ي

Alef ا (without the *Hamza* symbol ء), *Waw* و , and *Yaa* ي . This is like the English Language (aa -oo – ee). See examples in the following table:

Translation	Phonetics	مِثال	مِثال	المَدّ
Door	Baab	باب	ب + ا = با	المَدُّ بِالأَلِف:
Water	Maa'	ماء	م + ا = ما	
Book	Ketaab	كِتاب	ت + ا = تا	
Horse	Hesaan	حِصان	ص + ا = صا	
Market	Sooq	سوق	س + و = سو	المَدُّ بِالواو:
Cup	Koob	كوب	ك + و = كو	
Light	Noor	نور	ن + و = نو	
Box	Sondooq	صُنْدوق	د + و = دو	
In	Fee	في	ف + ي = في	المَدُّ بِالياء:
Kilo	Keelo	كيلو	ك + ي = كي	
Milk	Haleeb	حَليب	ل + ي = لي	
Shirt	Qamees	قَميص	م + ي = مي	

Note: Two Alefs cannot be written next to each other. Therefore, there's a sign (a little wave) that is put on top of the Alef to indicate that it is prolonged by a long vowel ا . It is written like this: آ = ا + أ

Now practice pronouncing all the Alphabets with the long vowels.

Congratulations! Now you know all that you need to learn to read and write Arabic. Now let's have a look at the main differences between Classical and Colloquial Arabic.

The Classical and The Colloquial

Most of the Colloquial words are a lighter form of the Classical. Changes are usually to avoid heavy letters such as ق ظ ذ ج ث , and grammatically sound rules (Parsing) and correct short vowels on the end of words are not really observed.

As there are 22 Arab Countries spread between different regions, there is a difference in dialects between countries, and sometimes also within each country. The colloquial words chosen in this book are the most popular and are perfectly understood everywhere.

With these simple rules you will know how to transfer the Classical to Colloquial:

Changing letters to lighter forms:

Classical	Colloquial	Examples
ث	ت	ثَعْلَب = تَعْلَب
ج	G As in good	جَمَل = Gamal
ذ	ز Or د	ذَكِّي = زَكِي ذَيْل = ديل
ظ	ز Heavier than the normal ز Or ض	ظَريف = زَريف ظُفْر = ضُفْر
ق	أ Or G (as in good)	قَمَر = أَمَر قَلْب = Galb
ك	تش Ch	كيس = تشيس

It is usually admirable if you want to speak in Classical Arabic/MSA when talking to people speaking in Colloquial. Yet understanding how dialects are developed would still be very beneficial for better communication.

The different Arabic dialects have many words in common. On the occasion that there is a strong difference, you will find three versions of the world listed in the order of Egyptian, Gulf, then Levant dialect. Sometimes it is only the Egyptian dialect that differs, in this case the versions for Gulf and Levant will be grouped together.

Being well-known for its light and popular dialect, Egypt is also famous for its ancient history, with Luxor alone having a third of the world's ancient monuments. Besides being the most populated Arab Country, it also has a very special Geographical position; a Mediterranean country that lies in North Africa, with a part of it in Asia (Sinai). Egypt is very famous for its touristic attractions, TV and Film productions, music, and arts.

The Levant and Gulf regions each have distinguished features and dialects of their own. They are both very rich in amazing touristic attractions, great historical and holy sites, and significant cultures. The well-known distinctive music and art productions and rapidly growing TV and film industries are also a very distinctive feature in both regions. The Gulf region especially is also known for wide business opportunities that attract many expatriates.

There is also the North African dialect, which may be harder to learn. However, the other dialects are understood perfectly in this region. North Africa is an astonishing region known for its rich history, unique touristic attractions (including skiing), strong culture, exclusive fashion, art, renowned architecture, and cuisine. Many movies are filmed in North Africa, especially in the Ouarzazate city of Morocco.

This is a general summary of letters modification from Classical to Colloquial:

1. ث is pronounced ت in many Arab countries except for the Gulf area.
2. ج is pronounced as it is (Jeem) in most Arab countries except for most parts of Egypt and parts of north Africa (pronounced g).
3. ذ is pronounced ز mainly in Egypt and some of the Levant area Countries. And pronounced as د in other North African countries.
4. ظ is pronounced as a heavier ز in Egypt and parts of the Levant area . It remains as it is in most of the Gulf area and becomes ض in parts of North Africa.
5. ق is pronounced أ in Egypt and the Levant area, and pronounced g in Sudan, parts of North Africa and the Gulf Region.
6. ك is pronounced Ch تش in Kuwaiti dialect.

To modify a Classical text into Colloquial:

1. Sound Grammatical rules are not really followed and correct short Vowels at the end of words are not observed. Usually *Sokoon* ْ and *Kasra* ِ are used at the end of words, and *Tanween* is very rarely used.

2. Change the heavy letters into lighter letters of your preferred dialect.

3. Use the popular Colloquial words suggestions in the book and in the end of the book.

And that's it! You can now move easily between the Classical/Modern Standard Arabic version and the Colloquial whenever you want.

Writing practice

Practice writing by tracing these words which you studied before:

أُخْت	أَخ	أَب	أُمّ
جَدَّة	جَدّ	بِنْت	وَلَد
قَلْب	حُبّ	ضَيْف	بَيْت
نور	قَمَر	شَمْس	خَيْر
بَرْد	حَرّ	بَحْر	بَرّ
جَيْب	عَيْن	وَجْه	رَأْس
ظَرْف	صُنْدوق	قَلَم	كِتاب
ثَعْلَب	كَلْب	جَمَل	قِطّ
قِفْ	حَديد	قِفْل	باب
كيلو	سوق	بَيْن	سِرّ
عِنَب	رُزّ	قَميص	لَوْن
بُنّ	حَليب	ماء	كوب
وَرْد	صَيْد	ضَرَر	شَرّ

Chapter Two

Demonstrative Pronouns – Defining – The Masculine and the Feminine – Adjectives – Colours – Prepositions – Adverbs – Conjunctions.

In the previous chapter, you learned how to write and read in Arabic, and words were Singular Nouns. In this chapter you will learn more about Nouns: The Demonstrative Pronouns, the difference between the Defined and Undefined Nouns, the Masculine and the Feminine Nouns, Adjectives and Colours, Prepositions, Adverbs, and Conjunctions.

Make sure you are comfortable reading and writing at this point. Enjoy learning all the new words to form better and more diverse sentences and keep practicing.

Demonstrative Pronouns ضَمائِرُ الإشارَة

Words in Arabic have gender. Hence, Pronouns are either Masculine or Feminine and there is no separate word for 'it' in Arabic. The following tables show all the different Demonstrative Pronouns.

Proximate	Feminine	Masculine
Single	هَـٰذِهِ دي – هَيْدي	هَـٰذا دا – هَيْدا
Dual *Rarely used in Colloquial*	هاتانِ	هَـٰذانِ
Plural	هَـٰؤُلاءِ دول – هادول	هَـٰؤُلاءِ دول – هادول
Remote	Feminine	Masculine
Single	تِلْكَ دي	ذَٰلِكَ دا
Dual *Rarely used in Colloquial*	تانِكَ	ذانِكَ
Plural *Rarely used in Colloquial*	أُولئِكَ	أُولئِكَ

<table>
<tr><td colspan="2" align="center">Places   الأماكِن</td></tr>
<tr><td align="center">Proximate</td><td align="center">هُنا

هِنا – هون</td></tr>
<tr><td align="center">Remote</td><td align="center">هُناك

هِناك – هونيك</td></tr>
</table>

Notes:

- *The Colloquial used in here is the Egyptian and the Levant dialects as the Gulf dialect is like the classical words in the first row, and for the rest, colloquial word suggestions can be used.*

- هذا – هذِهِ *: The letter Ha* ه *is prolonged by a long vowel* ا *(aa) , but it is not written. It is pronounced: Haatha – Haathehi. A small* ا *is written to indicate this.*

- ذٰلِكَ *: The letter thal* ذ *is prolonged by a long vowel* ا *(aa) but it is not written. So, it is pronounced: Thaalika. A small* ا *is written to indicate this. Same for* أُولٰئِكَ *.*

- *In Colloquial, the differences in Dual and Plural, near and far, are not really observed.* دول – هادول / هاذول *Dool/Hadool are usually used for all Dual and Plural near and far.*

Exercise 10: Practice using Singular Demonstrative Pronouns to describe the pictures below.

Object	English and phonetics	عَرَبي
	This is a pen. Haatha Qalam (Clss) *Da/Hayda Alam/Galam (Clq)* **The pen is here** Al-Qalamo Hona (Clss) *El-Alam/Galam Hena /Hoon (Clq)*	هَـٰذا قَلَم القَلَمُ هُنا
	That is a book. Thalika Kitaab (Clss) *Da/Hayda Kitaab (Clq)* **The book is there** AlKetabo Honak (Clss) *ElKetab Henaak /Honeek (Clq)*	ذَٰلِكَ كِتاب الكِتابُ هُناك
		....
		....

Defining tools   التَّعْريف

There are 5 ways to define a Noun in Arabic:

إسْمُ العَلَم – المُعَرَّف بِ ال – أَسْماءُ الإشارَة – الأَسْماءُ المَوْصولَة – الضَّمائِر – المُعَرَّف بالإضافَة

1. **The proper Noun** إسْمُ العَلَم : Specific Names of people, or places.

Examples:

Names of people: آدَم – زَيْنَب – جون – مايْكِل – سُمَيَّة

Names of places: بريطانْيا – مِصْر – باريس – عُمان – نيو يورك

2. **The Noun defined with Al** ال . This is the most basic way of defining.

3. **Demonstrative Pronouns**   أَسْماءُ الإشارَة: (هذا – هذه ......)

4. **Relative Pronouns**   الأَسْماءُ المَوْصولَة: (الَّذي – الَّتي ......)

5. **Personal Pronouns**   ضمائِرُ المُتكَلِّم – المُخاطَب – الغائِب (أَنا – أَنْتَ – هُوَ – هِيَ ......)

6. **The Genitive** المُعَرَّف بالإضافَة : When there are two Nouns next to each other, one
    without ال and the second with ال . This is used for Possession. In this case, the first
    word is identified by its connection to the second one: The man's name, the girl's
    bag, the car's colour, etc.:

إسْمُ الرَّجُل – حَقيبةُ البِنْت – لَوْنُ السَّيّارَة

Let us study each type in detail:

Defining with Al ال (The)

ال التَّعْريف

In Arabic, the definite article *Al* ال (*El* إل *in Colloquial*) is used as a Prefix to define Nouns. It is like (The) in English. The Article ال is affixed to Nouns and not to Verbs (This **is considered an important means to differentiate between a Noun and a Verb in Arabic**).

Sometimes the letter ل is not pronounced although it is written. This depends on the letter following it (the letter which the original Noun starts with).

There are two Groups of letters in Arabic: **Sun letters and Moon letters**:

- A word that starts with a Sun letter will have a *Shadda* ّ (stress) on its first letter which comes after ال. **The ل here will be written but silent**. An example of this is the word شمس (Sun), when defined, it is pronounced *Ash-shams* with a silent *lam* ل while written الشَّمْس

- A word that starts with a Moon letter will have one of the three short vowels (*Fat7a* َ – *Dhamma* ُ – *Kasra* ِ) on its first letter, and the ل here will be pronounced. An example for this is the word قَمَر (Moon), when defined, it is pronounced *AlQamar* القَمَر with a pronounced *Lam* ل.

Here is more on the Sun and Moon letters:

The Sun and the Moon Letters

ال الشَّمْسِيَّة و ال القَمَرِيَّة

You will find that the letter ل in ال naturally goes silent when pronouncing a word with a Sun letter, it will feel difficult to pronounce the ل in this case while it's easily pronounced with a Moon letter. So, there is no need to memorise the Sun and Moon letters as you will know them with practice. The *Shadda* ّ (stress) on the letter after ال is an easy way to recognise the Sun letters, while Moon letters will have *Fat7a* َ, *Dhamma* ُ , or *Kasra* ِ .

The 14 Sun letters are:

ت   ث   د   ذ   ر   ز   س   ش   ص   ض   ط   ظ   ل   ن

The 14 Moon letters are:

أ   ب   ج   ح   خ   ع   غ   ف   ق   ك   م   ه   و   ي

Now practice defining the Nouns you learnt so far by adding ال and then try forming short sentences with them.

Example:

- The girl is in the house   AlBento fee-AlBayt   البِنْتُ في البَيْت .
- The moon light   Nooro-AlQamar   نورُ القَمَر .

Important Note: In Arabic there is no **verb to be**. Therefore, (is) doesn't get translated into Arabic.

Exercise 11: Translate the short sentences below.

The Tea and the milk ---

The book is in a box ---

-- كِتابُ البِنْت

-- ضَيْفٌ في البَيْت

Exercise 12: Define these Nouns with ال and then read them correctly by noticing whether the letter ل is pronounced or silent, and then put these words into sentences.

ال القَمَرِيَّة	ال الشَّمْسِيَّة	The sentence الجُمْلَة	Translation	الكَلِمَة
			Man	رَجُل
			Woman	مَرْأَة
			Boy	وَلَد
			Girl	بِنْت
			Sky	سَماء
			Earth	أَرْض
			Fire	نار
			Water	ماء
			Air	هَواء
			Sand	تُراب

Exercise 13: Practice reading and writing these words, find their meanings and then decide which of them are defined.

حِصانُ البَحْر   لَنْدَن   سَيَّارةُ جون

صُنْدوقُ أَخي   الحَجَر   قِطَّة

شاي   كوبُ الماءِ   قَلَم

بَيْتُ الجَدّ   فَرَنْسا   القَمَر

The Masculine and the Feminine Nouns   المُذَكَّرُ وَ المُؤَنَّث

In Arabic, words are either Masculine or Feminine. Some Nouns hold the Gender naturally, for example: Sea بَحْر , Moon قَمَر , Light نور , Hospital مُسْتَشْفى , House بَيْت are always Masculine. And: موسيقى Music , صَحْراء Desert , شَمْس Sun , شَجَرَة Tree , أَرْض Land , are always Feminine.

Other Nouns can be either Masculine or Feminine, and these can be identified by the letter *Taa Marboota* ة at the end of the Singular Noun.

The basic rule is: Any singular word that ends with ة is Feminine.

The Feminine Noun (in most cases) consists of:

The Masculine Noun + Taa Marboota ة = The Feminine Noun.

طَبيب + ة = طَبيبَة

In this table, you will find the Masculine and the Feminine forms of Professions:

Profession	Transliteration	Profession مُؤَنَّث Feminine	Transliteration	Profession مُذَكَّر Masculine
Worker	3amela	عامِلَة	3amel	عامِل
Employee	MowaTh-thafa	مُوَظَّفَة	MowaTh-thaf	مُوَظَّف
Teacher	Modarresah	مُدَرِّسَة	Modarres	مُدَرِّس
Engineer	Mohandesa	مُهَنْدِسَة	Mohandes	مُهَنْدِس
Doctor	Tabeebah	طَبيبَة	Tabeeb	طَبيب
Police Officer	Shorteyyah	شُرْطِيَّة	Shorteyy	شُرْطِيّ
Manager	Modeerah	مُديرَة	Modeer	مُدير
Actor/Actress	Momath-thelah	مُمَثَّلَة	Momath-thel	مُمَثِّل

| Lawyer | Mo7ameyya | مُحامِيَة | Mo7amee | مُحامي |
| Player | La3eba | لاعِبَة | La3eb | لاعِب |

Note: As mentioned in the Beginning of the book when studying the Alphabet Group 2, Taa Marboota ة is pronounced as a Ha ه if the word stands alone or lies at the end of speaking. But when ة is followed by another word, it is pronounced as a Taa ت with any short Vowel.

Exercise 14: Create short sentences for these pictures and change the gender if possible.

Adjectives   الصِّفات

In Arabic, Adjectives come after the Noun and is identical to it in Gender, Number, Parsing (الرَّفْعُ و النَّصْبُ و الجَرّ) حَرَكاتُ الإعْراب and in being Defined or Undefined.

Adjective forms

There are different forms of Adjectives in Arabic. These are the most popular generic forms, and we will go through each one in detail.

Adjective **Feminine**	Adjective **Masculine**
فَعيلَة	فَعيل
فاعِلَة	فاعِل
فَعْلانَة	فَعْلان
فَعْلاء See colours	أَفْعَل See colours

Note: There are other Adjective forms. Two of which you will study in the following sections of the book: **The Object Form in the Verbs section, and the Relative Adjective.**

Adjective form Fa3eel   فَعيل

This is a very popular Adjective form. The table below contains examples of words and their opposites. The Feminine Adjectives are created by adding *Taa Marboota* ة to the Masculine word. You will also find the root Noun of each word.

Root Noun المَصْدَر	Translation	Adjective Feminine	Adjective Masculine
		فَعيلَة	فَعيل
Size كِبَر	Big	كَبيرَة	كَبير
Smallness صِغَر	Small	صَغيرَة	صَغير
Tallness طول	Tall	طَويلَة	طَويل
Shortness قِصَر	Short	قَصيرَة	قَصير
Fatness سِمْنَة	Fat	سَمينَة	سَمين
Thinness نَحافَة	Thin	نَحيفَة	نَحيف
Beauty جَمال	Beautiful	جَميلَة	جَميل
Ugliness قُبْح	Ugly	قَبيحَة	قَبيح
Distance بُعْد	Far	بَعيدَة	بَعيد
Proximity قُرْب	Near	قَريبَة	قَريب
Heaviness ثِقَل	Heavy	ثَقيلَة	ثَقيلَ

Lightness	خِفَّة	Light	خَفِيفَة	خَفِيف
Strength See Note	قُوَّة	Strong	قَوِيَّة	قَوِيّ
Weakness	ضَعْف	Weak	ضَعِيفَة	ضَعِيف
Speed	سُرْعَة	Fast	سَرِيعَة	سَرِيع
Slowness	بُطْء	Slow	بَطِيئَة	بَطِيء
Generosity	كَرَم	Generous	كَرِيمَة	كَرِيم
Stinginess	بُخْل	Stingy	بَخِيلَة	بَخِيل
Newness	تَجْدِيد	New	جَدِيدَة	جَدِيد
Oldness	قِدَم	Old	قَدِيمَة	قَدِيم

Note: Remember that a letter with Shadda ّ is considered two letters, therefore, the word قَوِيّ is a four letters Adjective.

See examples and practice writing:

شَجَرَةٌ طَوِيلَةٌ وَ شَجَرَةٌ قَصِيرَةٌ

طَرِيقٌ طَوِيلٌ

Adjective Form Fa3el فَاعِل

This is the second Adjective form. The Feminine Adjectives are created by adding *Taa Marboota* ة to the Masculine word. You will also find the root Noun of each word.

Root Noun المَصْدَر	Translation	Adjective Feminine	Adjective Masculine
Deed فِعْل	Doer	فاعِلة	فاعِل
Heat سُخونَة	Hot	ساخِنَة	ساخِن
Coldness بُرودَة	Cold	بارِدَة	بارِد

Note: This form is also used for the Subject Form (The doer of the Verb) such as:

Worker عامِل – Student طالِب – Player لاعِب .

Exercise 15: Describe these images using Adjectives that you learnt. Try to form as many words as you can in your sentences.

Adjective form Fa3lan   فَعْلان

This form is Created by adding two letters to a three letters Noun. The two letters added are the long vowel *Alef* ا and the letter ن (= ان). This will create the Masculine form of the Adjective. *Taa Marboota* ة is then added for the Feminine form. You will also find the root Noun of each word

Root noun المَصْدَر	Translation	Adjective **Feminine**	Adjective **Masculine**
		فَعْلانَة	فَعْلان
Heat (weather) حَرّ	Hot	حَرّانَة	حَرّان
Coldness بَرْد	Cold	بَرْدانَة	بَرْدانَ
Hunger جَوْع	Hungry	جَوْعانَة	جَوْعان
Thirst عَطَش	Thirsty	عَطْشانَة	عَطْشان

Notes:

- *A stress (شَدَّة) is considered Two letters in Arabic.*

- *Some Adjectives can come in two different forms. For example: Angry can come as غاضِب or غَضْبان , which is the form فاعِل or the form فَعْلان . In this case, the latter form (فَعْلان) is an Exaggeration form of the Adjective صيغَةُ مُبالَغَة .*

Exercise 16: Create the Masculine and the Feminine Adjectives in the Form فَعْلان for the following Nouns, and then put them into sentences.

نَدَم	سَهَر	كَسَل	زَعَل	فَرَح	غَضَب

Example:

الجَدُّ غَضْبانٌ في البَيْت.

الجَدّةُ غَضْبانَةٌ في البَيْت.

Colours   الألْوان

Colour in Feminine اللَّونُ المُؤَنَّث	English	Colour in Masculine اللَّونُ المُذَكَّر
حَمراء	Red	أحْمَر
بُرْتُقالِيَّة	Orange	بُرْتُقالي
صَفْراء	Yellow	أصْفَر
خَضْراء	Green	أخْضَر
زَرْقاء	Blue	أزْرَق
بَنَفْسَجِيَّة	Purple	بَنَفْسَجِيّ
وَرْدِيَّة	Pink	وَرْدي
رَمادِيَّة	Grey	رَمادي
بُنِّيَّة	Brown	بُنِّيّ
فِضِّيَّة	Silver	فِضِّيّ
ذَهَبِيَّة	Gold	ذَهَبِيّ
بَيْضاء	White	أبْيَض
سَوْداء	Black	أسْوَد

Exercise 17: Use Colours to describe these pictures. Use as much words as you can, such as Pronouns and Adjectives.

Example:

This is a thin man, and a big and heavy orange bag.

هذا رَجُلٌ نَحيفٌ و حَقيبَةٌ بُرْتُقالِيَّةٌ كَبيرَةٌ وَ ثَقيلَة.

Prepositions, Adverbs and Conjunctions

حروفُ الجَرّ- ظَرْفُ المَكان و ظَرْفُ الزَّمان – حُروفُ العَطْف

In this section we will study Prepositions, Adverbs, and Conjunctions.

1: Prepositions   حُروفُ الجَرّ

These are tools preceding a Noun. The following Noun will always be *Majroor* إِسْم مَجْرور .
Therefore, in most cases it will have *Kasra* ◌ِ كَسْرَة or *Tanween Bel-Kasr* ◌ٍ **if it is** تَنْوين بِالكَسْر
Singular. The first group of Prepositions are detached:

1: Detached Propositions   حُروفُ الجَرّ المُنْفَصِلَة

Translation	Examples	حُروفُ الجَرّ
From	الخَشَبُ مِنْ الشَّجَرِة Wood is from the tree	مِنْ
To	مِنَ الصَّباحِ إلى المَساءِ From the morning to the evening	إلى
About	دَرْسٌ عَن العَمَلِ A lesson about work	عَنْ
On	الصُّنْدوقُ عَلى الطّاوِلَةِ The box is on the table	عَلى
In	أَنا في البَيْتِ I am in the house	في

Note: عَلى – إلى *(pronounced Ela – 3ala) both end with* (ى) أَلِف مَقْصورَة *which is the long
vowel* ا *written as a* ى *(without the two dots).*

Exercise 18: Practice reading and writing the previous sentences in the table.

2: Attached Prepositions حُروفُ الجَرِّ المُتَّصِلَة

The second Group of Prepositions are attached. They are one letter each and they are affixed to the following word. The following Noun will always be *Majroor* إسْم مَجْرور. Therefore, in most cases it will have *Kasra* ِ kasra كَسْرَة or *Tanween Bel-Kasr* ٍ تَنْوين بِالكَسْر **if it is Singular**.

Preposition	Examples	حُروفُ الجَرِّ
with	شاي بِحَليب Tea with milk	بِ
Like	جَميلَةٌ كَالقَمَرِ Beautiful like the moon	كَ زَيّ
For	See Note حِزامُ الكُرْسِيِّ لِلسَّلامَةِ The seat belt is for safety	لِ

Note: The word لِلسَّلامَة consists of: للسَّلامَة = السَّلامَة + لِ *. When the letter* لِ *joins a word that starts with* ال*, the first letter* ا *(which is silent) is omitted.*

Exercise 19: Practice reading and writing the sentences in the table and try creating your own.

There are two types of Adverbs in Arabic: **Place Adverbs** and **Time Adverbs.** Place and Time Adverbs answer questions about Where and When. A Noun usually comes after an Adverb, and it is called a Genitive مُضاف / مُضاف إليه مَجرور . Therefore, in most cases it will have *Kasra* ِ كَسْرَة or *Tanween Bel-Kasr* ٍ تَنْوين بِالكَسْر **if it is Singular**.

1: Place Adverbs   ظَرْفُ المَكان

These are the most used Place Adverbs. They all have a *Fat7a* َ فَتْحَة at the end (except for few Adverbs that can be preceded by a Preposition, they don't have a *Fat7a* in the table). This is called مَبْني عَلى الفَتْح .

Place Adverb	Examples	ظَرْفُ المَكان
With	الوَلَدُ مَعَ الأُمُّ The boy is with the mother	مَعَ
At (place)	عِنْدَ البَيْتِ At home	عِنْدَ عَنْد
Above	فَوْقَ السَّطحِ Above the roof	فَوْقَ فوء – Foge
Under	تَحْتَ البَحْرِ Under the sea	تَحْتَ
In front of	السَّيارَةُ أمامَ المَنْزِلِ The car is in front of the house	أمامَ
Behind	الكُرَةُ خَلْفَ البابِ The ball is behind the door	خَلْفَ

Between	الطّاوْلَةُ بَيْنَ الكُرْسِيِّ وَ الكَنَبِة The table is between the chair and the sofa	بَيْنَ
Next to/Besides	الحَقيبَةُ بِجانِبِ البابِ The bag is besides the door	جانِب جَمْب
To the right of	السُّكَّرُ يَمينَ عُلْبَةِ الشّاي The sugar is on the right of the tea box	يَمين
To the left of	الكُرَةُ شِمالَ الكُرْسِيِّ The ball is on the left of the chair	شِمال - يَسار
Inside	الشّاي داخِلَ العُلْبَةِ The tea is inside the box	داخِلَ
Outside	القِطَّةُ خارِجَ البَيْتِ The cat is outside the house	خارِجَ

Exercise 20: Describe these pictures using Prepositions and Adverbs (look up any new words).

2: Time Adverbs   ظَرْفُ الزَّمان

These are the most used Time Adverbs. They all have *Fat7a* فَتْحَة ◌َ or *Tanween bel Fat7* ◌ً
تَنْوين بِالفَتْح at the end **except for the last four**, which may have different short vowels according to their position in the sentence.

Time Adverb	Examples	ظَرْفُ الزَّمان
Now	الآنَ الأَكْلُ جاهِز Now the food is ready	الآنَ دِلْوَأتي – اَلْحين
Before	قَبْلَ النَّوْمِ Before sleeping	قَبْلَ أَبْل – Gabl
After	بَعْدَ الأَكْلِ After eating	بَعْدَ
During	أَثْناءَ الغَداءِ During lunch	أَثْناءَ
Within	خِلالَ ساعَةٍ Within an hour	خِلالَ
Throughout	طَوالَ اليَوْمِ Throughout the day	طَوالَ طول
AM	السّابِعَةُ صَباحًا 7 AM	صَباحًا

PM	الثّامِنَةُ مَساءً 8 AM	مَساءً
The moment of	لَحْظَةُ الوِلادَةِ The moment of birth	لَحْظَة
The hour of	ساعَةُ الغُروبِ The sunset hour	ساعَة
The day of	يَوْمُ الأَحَدِ Sunday	يَوْم
The year of	سَنَةُ التَّخَرُّجِ The year of graduation	سَنَة - عام

Exercise 21: Translate the following by using the correct Time Adverbs. Look up new words.

During the meeting --

The year of the tiger (Chinese year) ---

Before the dawn ---

After the tea ---

All day long /Throughout the day--

Saturday ---

Food is at 6 AM ---

Dinner is within an hour --

The medicine is after the food ---

Reading is before sleeping --

These are the Arabic Conjunctions. The word following a Conjunction (except for حَتّى) will have the same sign of parsing الإعْراب as the word before the Conjunction. So it will be the same in terms of *Raf3* الرَّفْع , *Nasb* النَّصْب, and *Jarr* الجَرّ .

English	Examples	حَرْفُ العَطْف
And	قَلَمٌ وَ وَرَقَةٌ Pen and paper	وَ
Or For doubt For choice	هذا قَلَمٌ أَزْرَقٌ أَوْ أَسْوَدٌ This is a blue or a black pen بالسَّيَّارَةِ أوِ القِطارِ With the car or the train	أَوْ
Or To specify	الجَوُّ حارٌّ أَمْ بارِدٌ؟ The weather is hot or cold?	أَمْ وَلّا
But	لَيْسَ اليَوْمُ بَلْ غَدًا Not today but tomorrow	بَلْ Not used in colloquial
And then Short interval	الصَّغيرُ فَالكَبيرُ The young then the old	فَ Not used in colloquial
And then Long interval	حَسَن ثُمَّ آدَم Hassan and then Adam	ثُمَّ بَعْدين
Until **In order to** **Even**	حَتّى المَساء Until the evening أَنامُ حَتّى أَرْتاح I sleep in order to rest حَتّى أَنْتَ! Even you!	حَتّى لِحَدّ عَشان حَتّى

Not	الأَحْمَرُ لا الأَخْضَرُ The red not the green	لا مِش – مو
But (*Pronounced Laaken*)	القَميصُ جَميلٌ لكِنْ قَصيرٌ The shirt is beautiful but short	لٰكِنْ

Notes:

- بَلْ *is usually omitted altogether in colloquial.* لٰكِنْ *may be used instead.*
- فَ *is not used in colloquial* بَعْدين *is usually used instead.*

Exercise 22: Fill in the spaces with the right word.

البَرُّ --------------- البَحْرُ .   (لكِن – وَ – حَتَّى)

--------------- الصَّباح .   (لا – حَتَّى – وَ)

البَيْتُ كَبير --------------- بَعيد .   (أوْ – فَ – لكِن)

لَيْسَ هذا --------------- ذلِك .   (ثُمَّ – فَ – بَل)

القَصير --------------- الطَّويل .   (ثُمَّ – بَل – لكِن)

الوَرْدُ أَحْمَرُ --------------- أَصْفَر؟   (وَ – أَم – حَتَّى)

الحَقيبةُ الخَفيفَةُ --------------- الثَّقيلَة .   (بَل – لا – لكِن)

--------------- هُوَ في الخارِج؟   (أَم – ثُمَّ – حَتَّى)

This is the end of Part 1. Well done for reaching this far. Now you know how to read, write, and compose simple sentences using Singular Nouns, Demonstrative Pronouns, Prepositions, Adverbs, and Conjunctions. It is best to go through Part 1 again before starting Part 2.

In Part 2 you will learn about the Dual and the Plural forms, the rest of the Pronouns, Verbs, Nominal and Verbal sentences, the relative Adjective, Parsing, Negation tools, Numbers, Time, and Food and Beverage. You will also start writing Paragraphs and making Conversations.

We have designed a special Game for you to help you remember all the words you learned in this book, and to practice forming sentences in a fun way. This is called the Sentence Game, you will find the instructions and the words in a table at the end of Part 1 and Part 2, and you can play using all the words in both parts at the end of Part 2. All you need to do is to cut the words off the tables to form a playing Deck, and you can also laminate it yourself if you like. You will enjoy this game individually, and you will enjoy it even more in a group of 2 or more.

Enjoy your learning and see you in Part 2.

إلى اللِّقاء

The Sentence Game Instructions

Game Objective

The objective for each player is to use all their cards by forming sentences with a minimum of two cards per sentence. The first player to finish their cards wins the game.

Assembling The Sentence Game

Distribute the cards so that each player receives 14 cards, then place the remaining cards nearby, as this will be used during the game as a draw pile.

Rules

1. Every player, at the beginning of each turn, draws a word from the pile of cards. Then he tries to form as many sentences as possible with his cards and puts them down. If a player is unable to form any sentence with the drawn card, they pass.

2. If you have a blank card, you may use this in the place of any other word to form your sentence.

3. A player can use their turn to adapt previously formed sentences made by any other player. They can do this by:

● Adding one or more cards to the beginning, middle, or end of a sentence (as long as the produced sentence makes sense).

● Swapping out one word with another, then using the swapped card in a sentence of its own. Swapped cards must be used in the same turn.

● A player can also use the swapping method if the word they are swapping is a blank card, in which case they can change it to become a new word.

4. Once a player uses all their cards, the Game is over. Collect all the cards used in sentences and set them aside in a separate pile. You can then use the remaining card-drawing pile to begin a new game with different words.

5. Repeat this process until you have used all the words, then shuffle and start again.

The winner can now 'sentence' the losers with the verdict of their choosing ;)

Enjoy!

أَحْمَر	أَبْيَض	أَب
خَضْراء	أُخْت	أَخ
ال	ال	أَزْرَق
أَنا	إلى	ال
أَوْ	أَوْ	أَنا
أَمام	أُمّ	أَيْنَ
بارِد	بِ	أَمْريكا
بريطانْيا	بُرْتُقالي	بَحْر
بَعيدَة	بَرْدان	بَرْد

بِنْت	البَيْت	تَحْت
تِليفون	ة	ثَقيلَة
جَميلَة	جَوْعانَة	الجَوّ
حُبّ	حارّ	حَقيبَة
حَليب	خارِج	خَلْفَ
دُبَيْ	دولْفين	رَجُل
رَفيعَة	رُزّ	ساخِن
سُكَّر	سَلام	سَوْداء
سَيّارَة	السّينِما	شاي

شَجَرَة	شِمال	صَغير
ضَعيف	طَبيبَة	طَريق
طَويل	عَطْشانَة	عِنْد
في	في	الفيلْم
قَريبَ	قَصيرَة	قِطّ
قَلَم	قَليل	قَميص
كَبيرَ	كِتاب	كَريم
كوب	لِ	لَنْدَن
لَوْن	ماء	ماليزيا

مَع	مِن	مِن
نور	و	و
و	وَرْد	الوَلَد
هؤلاء	هذا	هذا
هذِهِ	هذِه	هُنا
هُناك	هُم	هُنَّ

Part 2

In Part 1 of the book, you learned how to read, write, and speak in Arabic. You learned about Nouns, Demonstrative Pronouns, Adjectives and Colours, Prepositions, Adverbs, and Conjunctions. And the focus was on the Singular form of words.

In Part 2, we will learn about the Dual and the Plural forms of words, and the rest of the Pronouns. You will also study Verbs in their past, present, future, and imperative tenses, and then you will learn how to form Verbal Sentences in addition to the Nominal Sentences you formed in Part 1. You will also study the Relative Adjective, Negation tools, Numbers and Time, Question tools, and Food and Beverage vocabulary, and you will then be fully capable of making conversations in Arabic. There will be Paragraph writing and Role play exercises to practice what you learned.

When you finish the book, you should be confident with your Arabic language in its Classical form, and you will also know how to transfer it smoothly to the Colloquial form. You will find **Audio files** to help you with pronunciation on our
website: **www.knowarabic.co.uk**, along with more interesting information about the Arabic language and history.

Enjoy your journey.

بِالتَّوْفيق

Singular, Dual and Plural Nouns

المُفْرَدُ و المُثَنّى وَ الجَمْع

All Nouns you studied so far were in the Singular form. We will now learn how to change the Singular into the Dual and the Plural forms.

The Dual form   صيغَةُ المُثَنّى

The Dual form is easily derived by adding two letters to the Singular Noun: The long Vowel *Alef* ا + *Noon* ن = ان . See examples for Dual Nouns in the state of **Raf3** in the following table:

المُثَنّى المَرْفوع:

Translation (Singular)	Dual المُثَنّى	Singular المُفْرَد
Man	رَجُلانِ	رَجُلٌ
Woman	مَرْأَتانِ	مَرْأَةٌ
Girl	بِنْتانِ	بِنْتٌ
Boy	وَلَدانِ	وَلَدٌ
House	بَيْتانِ	بَيْتٌ
car	سَيّارَتانِ	سَيّارَةٌ
Day	يَوْمانِ	يَوْمٌ
Hour	ساعَتانِ	ساعَةٌ

- *Tanween Beddham* ٌ (تَنْوين بالضَّم) is used for Singular words instead of *Dhamma* ُ (ضَمَّة) because the words stand alone.

- *Arraf3* (الرَّفْع) is <u>the original state of words</u>. Within sentences, Nouns are in *Raf3* state (مَرْفوعَة) when they are in the beginning of a Nominal sentence (مُبْتَدَأ) or a Subject (فاعِل) in the Verbal sentence. Present Verbs are also in *Raf3* state (مَرْفوعَة) in the start of Verbal sentences.

- If the **Dual word** is *Mansooba* (مَنْصوبَة) or *Majroora* (مَجْرورَة), the *Alef* ا turns into a *Yaa* ي . Within sentences, Nouns are in *Nasb* state (النَّصْب) mainly when they are an Object, (مَفْعول به) , and in *Jarr* state (الجَرّ) when preceded by Preposition, Adverb or a Genitive (مُضاف) .

Have a look at the following table to see how the words in the previous table change if they are **not** in the *Raf3* الرَّفْع state, which means they are either in *Nasb* النَّصْبُ or *Jarr* الجَرّ state:

المُثَنَّى المَنصوبُ أو المَجْرور:

Translation	Dual المُثَنَّى	Singular المُفْرَد
Man	رَجُلَيْنِ	رَجُلًا – رَجُلٍ
Woman	مَرْأَتَيْنِ	مَرْأَةً – مَرْأَةٍ
Girl	بِنْتَيْنِ	بِنْتًا – بِنْتٍ
Boy	وَلَدَيْنِ	وَلَدًا – وَلَدٍ
House	بَيْتَيْنِ	بَيْتًا – بَيْتٍ
car	سَيَّارَتَيْنِ	سَيَّارَةً – سَيَّارَةٍ
Day	يَوْمَيْنِ	يَوْمًا – يَوْمٍ
Hour	ساعَتَيْنِ	ساعَةً – ساعَةٍ

Notes:

The Tanween التَّنوين *is used here for Singular words instead of Fat7a* ◌َ *and* فَتْحَة
Kasra ◌ِ كَسْرَة *because the words stand alone.*

- *In colloquial Arabic, the Dual form which has* ين *is what is mainly used, and the letter*
before ين *will usually have Kasra:* رَجُلين – بِنْتين – وَلَدين – ساعْتين – يومين

The Plural form in Arabic is for any number above two. There are three Plural forms in Arabic:

1: The Sound Muscular Plural   جَمْعُ المُذَكَّرِ السّالِم

2: The Sound Feminine Plural   جَمْعُ المُؤَنَّثِ السّالِم

3: The Irregular Plural Form   جَمْعُ التَّكْسير

We will study each form separately.

1: Sound Masculine Plural   جَمْعُ المُذَكّرِ السّالِم

This Plural form is created by adding two letters to the Singular word:

- *Waw* and *Noon* ون in the state of *Raf3* الرَّفْع
- *Yaa* and *Noon* ين in the states of *Nasb* and *Jarr* النَّصْبُ وَالجَرّ

The following table has examples:

Translation (Singular)	Plural (ي + ن) الجَمْعُ في حالةِ النَّصْبِ أو الجَرّ	Plural (و + ن) الجَمْعُ في حالةِ الرَّفْع	Singular المُفْرَد
Visitor	زائِرين	زائِرون	زائِرٌ
Traveller	مُسافِرين	مُسافِرون	مُسافِرٌ
Believer	مُؤْمِنين	مُؤْمِنون	مُؤْمِنٌ
Player (Music)	عازِفين	عازِفون	عازِفٌ
Player (Games)	لاعِبين	لاعِبون	لاعِبٌ
Teacher	مُدَرِّسين	مُدَرِّسون	مُدَرِّسٌ
Engineer	مُهَنْدِسين	مُهَنْدِسون	مُهَنْدِسٌ
Farmer	مُزارِعين	مُزارِعون	مُزارِعٌ

2: Sound Feminine Plural جَمْعُ المُؤَنَّثِ السّالِم

This Plural form is created by replacing the letter *Taa Marboota* ة at the end of a Feminine word by the two letters *Alef* and *Taa* ات . The Plural word ends with *Dhamma* ُ /*Tanween Beddham* ٌ ضَمَّة تَنْوين بِالضَّم on the letter *Taa* ت in the case of *Raf3* الرَّفع, and *Kasra* ِ كَسْرة/*Tanween Bel-Kasr* ٍ تَنْوين بِالكَسر in the case of *Nasb* النَّصْب and *Jarr* الجَرّ . The following table has examples:

Translation (Singular)	Plural (ا + ت) الجَمعُ في حالة النَّصْبِ أو الجَرّ	Plural (ا + ت) الجَمعُ في حالَةِ الرَّفع	Singular المُفْرَد
Lady	سَيِّداتٍ	سَيِّداتٌ	سَيِّدَةٌ
Visitor	زائِراتٍ	زائِراتٌ	زائِرَةٌ
Traveller	مُسافِراتٍ	مُسافِراتٌ	مُسافِرَةٌ
Believer	مُؤْمِناتٍ	مُؤْمِناتٌ	مُؤْمِنَةٌ
Player (Games)	لاعِباتٍ	لاعِباتٌ	لاعِبَةٌ
Player (Music)	عازِفاتٍ	عازِفاتٌ	عازِفَةٌ
Teacher	مُدَرِّساتٍ	مُدَرِّساتٌ	مُدَرِّسَةٌ
Engineer	مُهَنْدِساتٍ	مُهَنْدِساتٌ	مُهَنْدِسَةٌ
Farmer	مُزارِعاتٍ	مُزارِعاتٌ	مُزارِعَةٌ
Worker	عامِلاتٍ	عامِلاتٌ	عامِلَةٌ
Beautiful	جَميلاتٍ	جَميلاتٌ	جَميلَةٌ

3: Irregular Plural form   جَمْعُ التَّكْسِير

This Plural form is used for both Males and Females. Unlike the previous forms, it doesn't follow a specific rule. Sometimes the Plural has more letters than the singular form and sometimes less letters. You get to know this Plural form by practicing the language. There are different forms for this Plural type, such as:

أَفْعال – فُعول – فِعال – فُعول – فُعَلاء – أَفْعُل – أَفْعِلاء – أَفاعِل – فُعُل

This Plural Form will have *Dhamma* ُ in *Raf3* state, *Fat7a* َ in *Nasb* state, and *Kasra* ِ in *Jarr* state **just like Singular Nouns**.

يُرفَعُ بِالضّمَّةِ و يُنْصَبُ بِالفَتْحَة وَ يُجَرُّ بِالكَسْرَة.

Check the following tables for examples:

1: The Plural has more letters than the Singular

Translation (Singular)	Plural الجَمْع	Singular المُفْرَد
Name	أَسْماء	إِسْم
Man	رِجال	رَجُل
Girl	بَنات	بِنْت
Boy	أَوْلاد	وَلَد
Person	أَشْخاص	شَخْص
Thing	أَشْياء	شَيْء
Number	أَرْقام	رَقَم
Day	أَيَّام	يَوْم
Week	أَسابيع	أُسْبوع
Month	شُهور	شَهْر
Year	أَعْوام	عام
Year	سِنين	سَنَة
Country	بِلْدان	بَلَد
Pen	أَقْلام	قَلَم
Cup	أَكْواب	كوب
Heart	قُلوب	قَلْب
Lesson	دُروس	دَرْس
Scholar /Scientist	عُلَماء	عالِم
Soldier	جُنود	جُنْدِيّ

Friend	أَصْدِقاء	صَديق
Companion	أَصْحاب	صاحِب
Chair	كَراسي	كُرْسي
Street	شَوارِع	شارِع
Paper	أَوْراق	وَرَقَة
Carrier bag	أَكْياس	كِيس
Shop	مَحَلّات	مَحَلّ
Restaurant	مَطاعِم	مَطْعَم
Currency	عُمْلات	عُمْلَة
Hand	أَيادي	يَد
Leg	أَرْجُل	رِجْل
Light	أَنْوار	نُور
Sea	بُحور	بَحْر
Dog	كِلاب	كَلْب
Strong	أَقْوِياء	قَوِيّ
Weak	ضُعَفاء	ضَعيف
Generous	كُرَماء	كَريم
Miserly	بُخلاء	بَخيل
Clever	أَذْكِياء	ذَكِيّ
Stupid	أَغْبِياء	غَبِيّ
Humorous	ظُرَفاء	ظَريف

2: The Plural has less letters than the Singular

Translation (Singular)	Plural الجَمْع	Singular المُفْرَد
Way	طُرُق	طَريق
Messenger	رُسُل	رَسول
Book	كُتُب	كِتاب
Egg	بَيْض بيض	بَيْضَة بيضَة
Box/Can	عُلَب	عُلْبَة
Toy	لُعَب	لُعْبَة
Brush	فُرَش	فُرْشاة فُرْشَه
White M-F	بيض	أَبْيَض – بَيْضاء
Black M-F	سود	أَسْوَد – سَوْداء
Red M-F	حُمْر	أَحْمَر – حَمْراء
Green M-F	خُضْر	أَخْضَر – خَضْراء
Blue M-F	زُرْق	أَزْرَق – زَرْقاء

That's it for the Plural forms. Now let us move onto studying Adjectives with the Plural Nouns, and then you will be able to form better sentences.

Using Adjectives with different Plural forms

As studied before, in the Arabic, the Adjective follows the word described, and is identical to
it in Gender, Identification, being Singular, Dual or Plural, and in Parsing marks عَلامات الإِعْراب
which means that it copies it in الرَّفْعُ وَ الضَّمُّ وَ الكَسْر .

<u>Describing Plural words:</u>

1. **For the first two Plural Forms:** جَمْعُ المُذَكَّرِ السّالِم – جَمْعُ المُؤَنَّثِ السّالِم

The **same form of Plural Adjectives** is used.

2. **For the third Plural Form:** جَمْعُ التَّكْسير

The **Singular Feminine Adjective Form** is used for describing the Non-Intelligent Irregular
Plural جَمْعُ التَّكْسيرِ غَيْرُ العاقِل like: dogs, chairs, boxes, etc. For the Intelligent Irregular Plural
جَمْعُ التَّكْسيرِ العاقِل like: men, friends, soldiers, etc., adjectives in all the Plural Forms can be
used.

See Examples:

<u>جَمْعُ المُذَكَّرِ السّالِم – جَمْعُ المُؤَنَّث السّالِم:</u>

مُدَرِّسونَ جَيِّدونَ

مُدَرِّساتٌ جَيِّداتٌ

الزّائِرونَ البريطانيّيون

الزّائِراتُ البريطانيّات

لاعِبونَ نَشيطونَ

لاعِباتٌ نَشيطاتٌ

الكَراسي الجَديدَةُ

الكِلابُ الضّالَةُ

قِطَطٌ صَغيرةٌ

شَوارِعٌ كَبيرَةٌ

بَناتٌ جَميلات

رِجالٌ أَقْوِياء – رِجالٌ كَثيرون

أَشْخاصٌ عُظَماء – أَشْخاصٌ قَليلون

Exercise 1: Turn the following words into the correct Plural form and then use suitable Adjectives to describe them. Try changing the words' gender when possible and form sentences using what you studied before.

طائِر– عامِل – طَبيبَة – قَلَم – مُوَظَّف – مُساعِد – دَرْس – مَدْرَسَة – طِفْل – مُدير – صُنْدوق – عُلْبَة

Personal Pronouns الضَّمائِرُ الشَّخْصِيَّة

Arabic Personal Pronouns are Detached words, and there are different Pronouns for the Singular, Dual, and Plural. For the First Person, Personal Pronouns are the same for both the Masculine and the Feminine speaker. For the **Second** and **Third Person**, Personal Pronouns are Gender sensitive for the Singular and Plural forms.

Important Note: The Masculine Dual and Plural Pronouns are used for Males only, or a mixture of Males and Females.

Personal Pronouns الضَّمائِرُ الشَّخْصِيَّة

Gender	Plural	Dual	Singular	
Masculine and Feminine	نَحْنُ We إِحْنا - نِحْنا	نَحْنُ We إِحْنا - نِحْنا	أَنا I	First Person
Masculine	أَنْتُم You إِنْتُو	أَنْتُما You إِنْتُو	أَنْتَ You إِنْتَ	Second Person
Feminine	أَنْتُنَّ You إِنْتُو	أَنْتُما You إِنْتُو	أَنْتِ You إِنْتِ	Second Person
Masculine	هُمْ They هُمّا	هُما They هُمّا	هُوَ He هُوَّ	Third Person
Feminine	هُنَّ They هُمّا - هِنّ	هُما They هُمّا	هِيَ She هِيَّ	Third Person

Possessive Pronouns   ضَمائِرُ المِلْكِيَّة

Arabic Possessive Pronouns are **Affixed Pronouns** consisting of one, two, or three letters that join to the end of a word. They differ according to the Gender and Number of the possessor.

In the following table you will find the Possessive Pronouns matching the Personal Pronouns you have just learnt. The word Book كِتاب (Noun) is used here as an example. However, Possessive Pronouns are affixed to Nouns, Verbs in all tenses, Prepositions, and Adverbs in the same way.

Singular Pronouns   ضَمائِرُ المُفْرَد

Example using كِتاب	Possessive Pronouns	ضَمائِرُ المِلْكِيَّة	Personal Pronouns	الضَّمائِرُ الشَّخْصِيَّة
كِتابي	My book	ي	I	أَنا
كِتابُكَ	Your book Male	كَ	**You** Male	أَنْتَ
كِتابُكِ	Your book Female	كِ	**You** Female	أَنْتِ
كِتابُهُ	His book	هُ	**He**	هُوَ
كِتابُها	Her book	ها	**She**	هِيَ

Dual Pronouns　　ضَمائِرُ المُثَنّى

كِتابُكُما	Your book Males/Females	كُما	You - Dual Male/Female	أَنْتُما
كِتابُهُما	Their book Males/Females	هُما	They - Dual Male/Female	هُما

Plural Pronouns　　ضَمائِرُ الجَمْع

كِتابُنا	Our book Males/Females	نا	We Males/Female	نَحْن
كِتابُكُمْ	Your book Males	كُمْ	You Males	أَنْتُمْ
كِتابُكُنَّ	Your book Females	كُنَّ	You Females	أَنْتُنَّ
كِتابُهُمْ	Their book Males	هُمْ	They Males	هُمْ
كِتابُهُنَّ	Their book Females	هُنَّ	They Females	هُنَّ

Note: For a group of two or more that has a mixture of males and females we use Masculine Pronouns.

Examples:

-My name is Malek, and his name is Zein.

أنا إِسْمي مالِك ، وَ هُوَ إِسْمُهُ زين.

-What is your name?

ما إِسْمُكَ؟ / ما إِسْمُكِ؟

-My name is Deena and my sister's name is Hana.

إِسْمي دينا وإِسْمُ أُخْتي هَنا.

-Your name is Sara?

إِسْمُكِ سارة؟

-They work at a restaurant that is called Milano.

هُم يَعْمَلونَ في مَطْعَمٍ إِسْمُهُ ميلانو.

-Here you go, this is your order.

تَفَضَّلْنَ، هذا طَلَبُكُنَّ.

This is their (Dual) father.

هذا أَبوهُما.

Exercise 2: Translate these sentences into Arabic using Personal Pronouns.

English	العَرَبِيَّة
I am at home.	
You are at home?	
He is in the market.	
She is at school.	
You both are on the way?	
	أَنْتُنَّ داخِلَ السّينِما؟
	أَنْتُمْ عِنْدَ المَطار؟
	هُمْ مِنَ العِراق.
	هُنَّ مِن فِلسْطين.

Exercise 3: Translate these sentences into Arabic using Demonstrative and Possessive Pronouns.

Example:

English	العَرَبِيَّة
This is their house.	هذا بَيْتُهم.
That is his shirt.	ذلِكَ قَميصُه.
Here! This is her cup.	هُنا ! هذا كوبُها.
That is her school.	
There! That is our car.	
This is your tea?	
My pen is here.	

Relative Pronouns الأَسْماءُ المَوصولَة

Relative Pronouns in Arabic are **Detached Pronouns**. There are different Pronouns for the Masculine and the Feminine, and for the Singular, Dual and Plural. This table shows the Relative Pronouns in the Classical and the Colloquial form (in Grey).

Relative Pronouns	الاسْتِخْدام	الأَسْماءُ المَوصولَة
Who/That/Which Single Masculine Intelligent and non-Intelligent	المُفْرَدُ المُذَكَّر العاقِلُ وَغَيْرُ العاقِل	الَّذي إلِّي
Who/That/Which Single Feminine. Intelligent and non-Intelligent Non-Intelligent Plural (Objects – Animals – Plants)	المُفْرَدُ المُؤَنَّث العاقِلُ وَغَيْرُ العاقِل <u>وَالجَمْعُ غَيْرُ العاقِل</u>	الَّتي إلِّي
Who/That/Which Dual Masculine Intelligent and non-Intelligent.	المُثَنَّى المُذَكَّر العاقِلُ وَغَيْرُ العاقِل	اللَّذانِ – اللَّذَيْنِ إلِّي
Who/That/Which Dual Feminine Intelligent and non-Intelligent.	المُثَنَّى المُؤَنَّث العاقِلُ وَغَيْرُ العاقِل	اللَّتانِ – اللَّتَيْنِ إلِّي
Who/That/Which Intelligent Masculine Plural	الجَمْعُ المُذَكَّر العاقِل	الَّذينَ إلِّي
Who/That/Which Intelligent Feminine Plural	الجَمْعُ المُؤَنَّث العاقِل	اللّاتي إلِّي

Who/That Single, Dual, and Plural. Intelligent Masculine and Feminine.	المُفْرَدُ وَ المُثَنَّى وَ الجَمْعُ **المُذَكَّرُ وَ المُؤَنَّث** العاقِل	مَنْ الِّي
What/That Single, Dual, and Plural. Masculine and Feminine. Mostly for the Non-Intelligent	المُفْرَدُ وَ المُثَنَّى وَ الجَمْعُ **المُذَكَّرُ وَ المُؤَنَّث** **غَيْرُ العاقِلِ غالِبًا** <u>تُستَخْدَم للعاقِلِ أَحْيانًا</u>	ما الِّي

Note: The Colloquial version is the same for all the Relative Pronouns. The word الِّي (Ellee) is used instead of all the Classical words in this table.

Examples

1. The man that's in the picture, is my father.

Classical: الرَّجُلُ الَّذي في الصّورَةِ هُوَ أَبي.

Colloquial: الراجِلِ الِّي في الصّورَه هُوَّ أَبويا.

Note: Demonstrative Pronouns like هُوَ in the previous example can be used like Verb (To Be) in the English language.

2. The two Cats that are on top of the roof are beautiful.

Classical:	القِطَّتانِ الَّلتانِ فَوْقَ السَّطْحِ جَميلَتانِ.
Colloquial:	الأُطَّتين اِلّي فوقِ السَّطْح جُمال.

3. Those toys that are on the shelves are my son's toys.

Classical:	تِلْكَ الُّلعَبُ الَّتي عَلى الرُّفوفِ لُعَبُ إبْني.
Colloquial 1:	اللِّعَبْ دي اِلّي على الرُّفوفْ لِعَبْ إبْني.
Colloquial 2:	هذي اللُّعَب اِلّي عَلى الرُّفوفْ لُعَبْ إبْني.

Notes:

1: تِلْكَ is not used in Colloquial Arabic (Demonstrative Pronouns studied in Part 1). Usually, هذي is used instead.

2: In the first Colloquial version (Egyptian), the word دي comes after the described Noun.

4. What comes after winter is spring.

Classical:	ما يَأْتي بَعْدَ الشِّتاءِ هُوَ الرَّبيع.
Colloquial:	اِلّي بييجي بَعْدِ الشِّتا هُوَّ الرَّبيع.

5. I like those who speak with honesty.

Classical:

أُحِبُّ مَنْ يَتَكَلَّمُ بِصِدْق.

Colloquial:

بَحِبّ اِلّي يِتْكَلّم بِصِدْء.

Exercise 4: Describe these images using Relative Pronouns. Write sentences like in the previous examples.

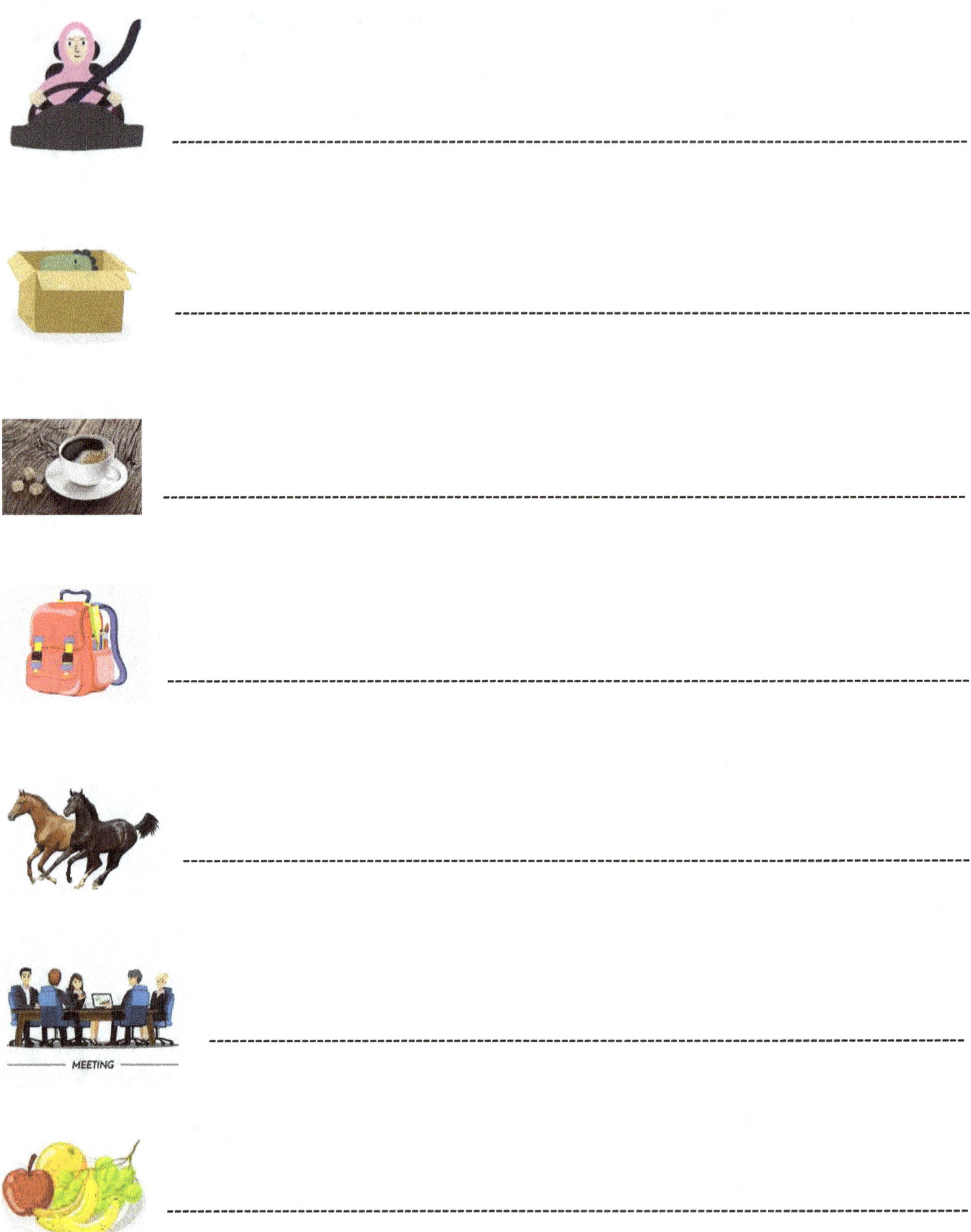

<h1 align="center">Verbs   الأَفْعَال</h1>

Now it is time to learn about **Verbs**. In this section, you will learn the Past, Present, and Imperative (Command) Tenses, and you will also learn the Subject and Object Forms.

Arabic has a very large number of Verbs of various forms, the Past Tense of the Verb is what determines the rest of the words stemming from it. Here we will cover the most used and popular forms.

Here is an easy method for building words from a Past Tense Verb in the **Singular Masculine**, which is considered the generic form.

Past – Present – Command – Subject – Object

<u>In this way you are learning:</u>

1. The Past, Present and Command Verbs' Forms
2. The Subject Form
3. The Object Form

Note that as mentioned in the Adjectives section, the Object form مَفْعُول is also a popular **Adjective form**. Like: مَعْروف – مَلْبوس – مَرْفوع – مَسْموع – مَحْبوب – مَشْهور

Here are some of the most used Verbs and their Conjugation method (the translation is in the table at the end):

1: Three letters Past tense فَعَلَ and the Present tense is يَفْعَلُ :

(This is the most generic Form)

فَعَلَ – يَفْعَلُ – اِفْعَلْ. فَهُوَ فاعِلٌ وَ المَفْعولُ مِنْهُ مَفْعولٌ.

Examples:

ذَهَبَ – فَتَحَ – قَرَأَ

ذَهَبَ – يَذْهَبُ – اِذْهَبْ. فَهُوَ ذاهِبٌ وَ المَفْعولُ مِنْهُ مَذْهوبٌ.

فَتَحَ – يَفْتَحُ – اِفْتَحْ. فَهُوَ فاتِحٌ وَ المَفْعولُ مِنْهُ مَفْتوحٌ.

قَرَأَ – يَقْرَأُ – اِقْرَأْ. فَهُوَ قارِئٌ وَ المَفْعولُ مِنْهُ مَقروءٌ.

2: Three letters Past tense فَعَلَ and the Present tense is يَفْعُلُ :

فَعَلَ – يَفْعُلُ – اِفْعَلْ. فَهُوَ فاعِلٌ وَ المَفْعولُ مِنْهُ مَفْعولٌ.

Examples:

دَخَلَ – خَرَجَ – طَلَبَ – كَتَبَ – أَخَذَ – أَكَلَ

دَخَلَ – يَدْخُلُ – اِدْخُلْ. فَهُوَ داخِلٌ وَ المَفْعولُ مِنْهُ مَدْخولٌ.

خَرَجَ – يَخْرُجُ – اِخْرُجْ. فَهُوَ خارِجٌ وَ المَفْعولُ مِنْهُ مَخروجٌ.

طَلَبَ – يَطْلُبُ – اِطْلُبْ. فَهُوَ طالِبٌ وَ المَفْعولُ مِنْهُ مَطْلوبٌ.

كَتَبَ – يَكْتُبُ – اِكْتُبْ. فَهُوَ كاتِبٌ وَ المَفْعولُ مِنْهُ مَكْتوبٌ.

Some Verbs that fall under this category start with *Hamza* أ like أَخَذَ - أَكَلَ . In this case the conjugation method remains the same except for the Command Verb, as the أ gets omitted for the ease of pronunciation:

أَخَذَ – يَأْخُذُ – خُذْ. فَهُوَ آخِذٌ و المَفْعول مِنْهُ مَأْخوذٌ.

أَكَلَ – يَأْكُلُ – كُلْ. فَهُوَ آكِلٌ وَ المَفْعولُ مِنْهُ مَأْكولٌ.

3: Three letters Past tense فَعَلَ and the Present tense is يَفْعِلُ :

فَعَلَ – يَفْعِلُ – اِفْعِلْ. فَهُوَ فاعِلٌ وَ المَفْعُولُ مِنْهُ مَفْعُولٌ.

Examples:

ضَرَبَ – مَسَكَ

ضَرَبَ – يَضْرِبُ – اِضْرِبْ. فَهُوَ ضارِبٌ وَ المَفْعُولُ مِنْهُ مَضْروبٌ.

مَسَكَ – يَمْسِكُ – اِمْسِكْ. فَهُوَ ماسِكٌ وَ المَفْعُولُ مِنْهُ مَمْسوكٌ.

4: Three letters Past tense فَعِلَ and the Present tense is يَفْعَلُ :

فَعِلَ – يَفْعَلُ – اِفْعَلْ. فَهُوَ فاعِلٌ و المَفْعُولُ مِنْهَ مَفْعُولٌ.

Examples:

سَمِعَ – شَرِبَ – عَمِلَ – فَهِمَ

سَمِعَ – يَسْمَعُ – اِسْمَعْ. فَهُوَ سامِعٌ وَ المَفْعُولُ مِنْهُ مَسْموعٌ.

شَرِبَ – يَشْرَبُ – اِشْرَبْ. فَهُوَ شارِبٌ و المَفْعُولُ مِنْهُ مَشْروبٌ.

عَمِلَ – يَعْمَلُ – اِعْمَلْ. فَهُوَ عامِلٌ و المَفْعُولُ مِنْهُ مَعْمولٌ.

فَهِمَ – يَفْهَمُ – اِفْهَمْ. فَهُوَ فاهِمٌ و المَفْعُولُ مِنْهُ مَفْهومٌ.

5: Four letters Past tense أَفَعَلَ and the Present tense is يُفْعِلُ :

أَفْعَلَ – يُفْعِلُ – أَفْعِلْ. فَهُوَ مُفْعِلٌ و المَفْعُولُ مِنْهُ مُفْعَلٌ.

Examples:

أَدْخَلَ – أَرْشَدَ

أَدْخَلَ – يُدْخِلُ – أَدْخِلْ. فَهُوَ مُدْخِلٌ و المَفْعُولُ مِنْهُ مُدْخَلٌ.

أَرْشَدَ – يُرْشِدُ – أَرْشِدْ. فَهُوَ مُرْشِدٌ و المَفْعُولُ مِنْهُ مُرْشَدٌ.

6: Four letters Past tense أَفْعَلَ and the third letter is a long vowel مَدٌّ بِالأَلِف

Examples:

أَرادَ – أَقامَ

أَرادَ – يُريدُ – أَرِدْ. فَهُوَ مُريدٌ وَ المَفْعُولُ مِنْهُ مُرادٌ.

أَقامَ – يُقيمُ – أَقِمْ. فَهُوَ مُقيمٌ وَ المَفْعُولُ مِنْهُ مُقامٌ.

7: Four letters Past tense أَفْعَلَ with a *Shadda* ـّ on the third letter (considered two letters):

Examples:

أَحَبَّ – أَعَدَّ

أَعَدَّ – يُعِدُّ – أَعِدَّ. فَهُوَ مُعِدٌّ وَ المَفْعُولُ مِنْهُ مُعَدٌّ.

أَحَبَّ – يُحِبُّ – أَحِبَّ. فَهُوَ مُحِبٌّ وَ المَفْعُولُ مِنْهُ مُحَبٌّ.

8: Five letters Past tense تَفَعَّلَ **and the Present tense is** يَتَفَعَّلُ :

تَفَعَّلَ – يَتَفَعَّلُ – تَفَعَّلْ. فَهُوَ مُتَفَعِّلٌ و المَفْعُولُ مِنْهُ مُتَفَعَّلٌ.

Examples:

تَعَلَّمَ – تَكَلَّمَ

تَعَلَّمَ – يَتَعَلَّمُ – تَعَلَّمْ. فَهُوَ مُتَعَلِّمٌ و المَفْعُولُ مِنْهُ مُتَعَلَّمٌ.

تَكَلَّمَ – يَتَكَلَّمُ – تَكَلَّمْ. فَهُوَ مُتَكَلِّمٌ وَ المَفْعُولُ مِنْهُ مُتَكَلَّمٌ.

For the **Feminine** Form of the Subject and Object Nouns, we just add ة and change the Short Vowel of the previous letter to فَتْحَة :

ذاهِبَةٌ مَذْهوبَةٌ – فاتِحَةٌ مَفْتوحَةٌ – قارِئَةٌ مَقْروءَةٌ – آخِذَةٌ مَأْخوذَةٌ – آكِلَةٌ مَأْكولَةٌ – داخِلَةٌ مَدْخولَةٌ – خارِجَةٌ مَخْروجَةٌ – طالِبَةٌ مَطْلوبَةٌ – كاتِبَةٌ مَكْتوبَةٌ – سامِعَةٌ مَسْموعَةٌ – شارِبَةٌ مَشْروبَةٌ – عامِلَةٌ مَعْمولَةٌ – فاهِمَةٌ مَفْهومَةٌ – مُدْخِلَةٌ مُدْخَلَةٌ – مُرْشِدَةٌ مُرْشَدَةٌ – مُريدَةٌ مُرادَةٌ – مُقيمَةٌ مُقامَةٌ – مُحِبَّةٌ مُحَبَّةٌ – مُعِدَّةٌ مُعَدَّةٌ – مُتَعَلِّمَةٌ مُتَعَلَّمَةٌ – مُتَكَلِّمَةٌ مُتَكَلَّمَةٌ

Here is a table of all the previous Verbs with the translation:

Translation التَّرْجَمَة	Object المَفْعُول به	Subject الفَاعِل	Command فِعْلُ الأَمْر	Present tense الفعل المُضارِع	Past tense الفِعْلُ الماضي
To go	مَذْهوب	ذاهِب	إذْهَبْ	يَذْهَبُ	ذَهَبَ
To open	مَفْتوح	فاتِح	إفْتَحْ	يَفْتَحُ	فَتَحَ
To read	مَقْروء	قارِئ	إقْرَأْ	يَقْرَأُ	قَرَأَ
To enter	مَدْخولُ	داخِل	إدْخُلْ	يَدْخُلُ	دَخَلَ
To go out	مَخْروج	خارِج	إخْرُجْ	يَخْرُجُ	خَرَجَ
To request	مَطْلوب	طالِب	إطْلُبْ	يَطْلُبُ	طَلَبَ
To write	مَكْتوب	كاتِب	إكْتُبْ	يَكْتُبُ	كَتَبَ
To take	مَأْخوذ	آخِذ	خُذْ	يَأْخُذُ	أَخَذَ
To eat	مَأْكول	آكِل	كُلْ	يَأْكُلُ	أَكَلَ
To hear	مَسْموع	سامِع	إسْمَعْ	يَسْمَعُ	سَمِعَ
To drink	مَشْروب	شارِب	إشْرَبْ	يَشْرَبُ	شَرِبَ
To do	مَعْمول	عامِل	إعْمَلْ	يَعْمَلُ	عَمِلَ
To understand	مَفْهوم	فاهِم	إفْهَم	يَفْهَمُ	فَهِمَ
To insert	مُدْخَل	مُدْخِل	إدْخُلْ	يُدْخِلُ	أَدْخَلَ
To guide	مُرْشَد	مُرْشِد	إرْشِدْ	يُرْشِدُ	أَرْشَدَ
To want	مُراد	مُرِيد	أَرِدْ	يُرِيدُ	أَرادَ
To set up	مُقام	مُقِيم	أَقِمْ	يُقِيمُ	أَقامَ
To love	مُحَبّ	مُحِبّ	أَحِبّ	يُحِبُّ	أَحَبَّ
To prepare	مُعَدّ	مُعِدّ	أَعِدّ	يُعِدُّ	أَعَدَّ
To learn	مُتَعَلّم	مُتَعَلّم	تَعَلّمْ	يَتَعَلّمُ	تَعَلّمَ
To speak	مُتَكَلّم	مُتَكَلّم	تَكَلّمْ	يَتَكَلّمُ	تَكَلّمَ

Exercise 5: Fill in the following table with the Verbs that you learnt, and then create sentences for them.

Examples:

هذا الدّاخِلُ إلى البَيْتِ هُوَ آدَم.

يَخْرُجُ أبي إلى العَمَل في الصَّباح.

تَكَلَّمَ في التّليفون.

أنا مُحِبَّةٌ لَكُمْ.

هُوَ يَعْمَلُ مُرْشِدٌ سِياحِيّ.

الصَّوْتُ مَسْموعٌ.

هذِهِ هِيَ كاتِبَةُ الكِتاب.

المَكانُ مُعَدٌّ لَكُمْ.

Note: لَكُم *means: For you in Plural.*

| Translation | Object | Subject | Command | Present tense | Past tense |
التَّرْجَمَة	المَفْعولُ بِه	الفاعِل	فِعْلُ الأَمْر	الفعلُ المُضارع	الفِعْلُ الماضي
					ذَهَبَ
					فَتَحَ
					قَرَأَ
					دَخَلَ
					خَرَجَ
					طَلَبَ
					كَتَبَ
					أَخَذَ
					أَكَلَ
					سَمِعَ
					شَرِبَ
					عَمِلَ
					فَهِمَ
					أَدْخَلَ
					أَرْشَدَ
					أَرادَ
					أَقامَ
					أَحَبَّ
					أَعَدَّ
					تَعَلَّمَ
					تَكَلَّمَ
التَّرْجَمَة	المَفْعولُ بِه	الفاعِل	فِعْلُ الأَمْر	الفعلُ المُضارع	الفِعْلُ الماضي

Your sentences:

Verbs Conjugation

تَصْريفُ الأَفْعال

Now that you know the Basic Past, Present, and Command Verbs, let us study how they differ according to all the Personal Pronouns you studied before.

1: Past Tense Conjugation   تَصْريفُ الفِعْلِ الماضي

Here is the Conjugation of the Past Tense Verbs according to the different Personal Pronouns. The basic generic Past tense Verb **فَعَلَ** is used here.

Past tense	Plural	Past tense	Dual	Past tense	Singular
فَعَلْنا	نَحْنُ	فَعَلْنا	نَحْنُ	فَعَلْتُ	أَنا
فَعَلْتُم	أَنْتُم	فَعَلْتُما	أَنْتُما	فَعَلْتَ	أَنْتَ
فَعَلْتُنَّ	أَنْتُنَّ	فَعَلْتُما	أَنْتُما	فَعَلْتِ	أَنْتِ
فَعَلوا See Note	هُمْ	فَعَلا	هُما	فَعَلَ	هُوَ
فَعَلْنَ	هُنَّ	فَعَلَتا	هُما	فَعَلَتْ	هِيَ

Notes:

- *Plural Past Tense Verbs always have an ا written after the و like this:* (وا) . *It is written but not pronounced. So,* فَعَلوا *is pronounced Fa3aloo.*

- *The same letters are added for the rest of **Past Tense forms** which you have studied before, except for Number 6 and 7:*

For Number 6: The long vowel is omitted:

أَرادَ – أَرَدْتُ – أَرَدْنا

أَقامَ – أَقَمْتُ – أَقَمْنا

For Number 7: The double letters contained in the Shadda⟡ is separated:

أَحَبَّ – أَحْبَبْتُ – أَحْبَبْنا

أَعَدَّ – أَعْدَدْتُ – أَعْدَدْنا

Exercise 6: Insert the right form for these Past Tense Verbs according to different Pronouns in the table below.

| أَدْخَلَ | سَمِعَ | طَلَبَ | دَخَلَ | قَرَأَ | ذَهَبَ |

Past tense	Plural	Past tense	Dual	Past tense	Singular
فَعَلْنا	نَحْنُ	فَعَلْنا	نَحْنُ	فَعَلْتُ	أَنا
فَعَلْتُم	أَنْتُم	فَعَلْتُما	أَنْتُما	فَعَلْتَ	أَنْتَ
فَعَلْتُنَّ	أَنْتُنَّ	فَعَلْتُما	أَنْتُما	فَعَلْتِ	أَنْتِ

فَعَلوا	هُم	فَعَلا	هُما	فَعَلَ	هُوَ
--------------		--------------		--------------	141
--------------		--------------		--------------	
--------------		--------------		--------------	
--------------		--------------		--------------	
--------------		--------------		--------------	
--------------		--------------		--------------	

فَعَلْنَ	هُنَّ	فَعَلَتا	هُما	فَعَلَتْ	هِيَ
--------------		--------------		--------------	
--------------		--------------		--------------	
--------------		--------------		--------------	
--------------		--------------		--------------	
--------------		--------------		--------------	
--------------		--------------		--------------	

2: Present and Future Tenses Conjugation   تَصْرِيفُ الفِعْلِ المُضارِعِ وَ فِعْلِ المُسْتَقْبَل

Present Verbs differ in their **first and last letters** according to the preceding Personal Pronouns. <u>**The first letters**</u> of Present Verbs can be put together to form the word أَنَيْتُ

أ ن ي ت

And for the **future Tense**, we just affix the letter س (= will) at the beginning of each Verb.

Present and Future Tense Verbs Conjugation according to Personal Pronouns:

Future Tense	Present Tense	Present Tense Generic Form	Personal Pronouns	
سَأَكْتُبُ	أَكْتُبُ	أَفْعَلُ		أَنا
سَنَكْتُبُ	نَكْتُبُ	نَفْعَلُ		نَحْنُ
سَيَكْتُبُ	يَكْتُبُ	يَفْعَلُ		هُوَ
سَيَكْتُبانِ	يَكْتُبانِ	يَفْعَلانِ	Masculine	هُما
سَيَكْتُبونَ	يَكْتُبونَ	يَفْعَلونَ		هُم
سَتَكْتُبُ	تَكْتُبُ	تَفْعَلُ		هِيَ
سَتَكْتُبانِ	تَكْتُبانِ	تَفْعَلانِ	Feminine	هُما
سَيَكْتُبْنَ	يَكْتُبْنَ	يَفْعَلْنَ		هُنَّ
سَتَكْتُبُ	تَكْتُبُ	تَفْعَلُ		أَنْتَ
سَتَكْتُبانِ	تَكْتُبانِ	تَفْعَلانِ	Masculine	أَنْتُما
سَتَكْتُبونَ	تَكْتُبونَ	تَفْعَلونَ		أَنْتُم
سَتَكْتُبينَ	تَكْتُبينَ	تَفْعَلينَ		أَنْتِ
سَتَكْتُبانِ	تَكْتُبانِ	تَفْعَلانِ	Feminine	أَنْتُما
سَتَكْتُبْنَ	تَكْتُبْنَ	تَفْعَلْنَ		أَنْتُنَّ

Notes:

- The same letters are added for the rest of the Past tense forms which you have studied before.

- For the Future tense in Colloquial: Instead of س you either add the letter هـ or ح أَنا هَخُرُج / أَنا راحَ اخْرُج (Egyptian dialect) or the word راح . So, instead of أَنا سَأَخْرُج you say: أَنا راحَ اخْرُج

Exercise 7: Write the Correct Present tense for the following Past tense Verbs according to Pronouns, and then create sentences for them.

أَحَبَّ	أَرادَ	شَرِبَ	ضَرَبَ	خَرَجَ	فَتَح	
						أَنا
						نَحْنُ
						هُوَ
						هُما
						هُم
						هِيَ
						هُما
						هُنَّ
						أَنْتَ
						أَنْتُما
						أَنْتُم
						أَنْتِ
						أَنْتُما
						أَنْتُنَّ

Example:

نَحْنُ نَجْلِسُ في المَطْعَم.

نَحْنُ نَجْلِسُ في المَطْعَم.

3: Imperative Tense Conjugation   تَصْريفُ فِعْلِ الأَمْر

Finally, the Imperative (Command) Tense. Here is the table for it:

Example مِثال	Command Verb فِعْلُ الأَمْر	Pronoun الضَّمير	
اِشْرَبْ	اِفْعَلْ	Male	أَنْتَ
اِشْرَبا	اِفْعَلا	Male	أَنْتُما
اِشْرَبوا	اِفْعَلوا	Male	أَنْتُم
اِشْرَبي	اِفْعَلي	Female	أَنْتِ
اِشْرَبا	اِفْعَلا	Female	أَنْتُما
اِشْرَبْنَ	اِفْعَلْنَ	Female	أَنْتُنَّ

Note: The same letters are added for the rest of the Verb forms which you have studied before. Verbs that start with أ like أَخَذَ – أَكَلَ will not have the ﺍ in the start: كُلْ – خُذْ

Now practice the Command Tense with the Verbs you have learned before:

Exercise 8: Write the Correct Command tense for the following Past tense Verbs according to the Pronouns, and then create sentences for them.

دَخَلَ	شَرِبَ	مَسَحَ	جَمَعَ	أَخَذَ	أَكَلَ	
					كُلْ	أَنْتَ
					كُلا	أَنْتُما
					كُلوا	أَنْتُم
					كُلي	أَنْتِ
					كُلا	أَنْتُما
					كُلْنَ	أَنْتُنَّ

Sentences for Command Verbs:

Example:

إِشْرَبْ الماء.

The Nominal and the Verbal sentence

الجُمْلَةُ الإِسْمِيَّةُ وَ الجُمْلَةُ الفِعْلِيَّة

In Arabic, content is expressed using either **Nominal** or **Verbal** sentences. Nominal sentences begin with a Noun, and Verbal Sentences begin with a Verb.

Nominal sentences

Nominal Sentences have Two Parts: A Defined Subject مُبْتَدأ and a Predicate خَبَر

In the simplest form of a Sentence, these Two parts are one word each.

1. The First Word is a **Defined Noun**:

مُبْتَدَأ مَرْفوع: بالضَّمَّةِ لِلْمُفْرَد، أَوَ بِالأَلِف لِلْمُثَنَّى، أَوْ بالواوِ لِلجَمْع .

2. The Second Word is an **Undefined Noun**:

خَبَر مَرْفوع: بِالتَّنْوينِ بِالضَّمِّ لِلْمُفْرَد، أَوْ بِالأَلِف لِلْمُثَنَّى، أَوْ بِالواوِ لِلجَمْع .

The second Part of the Sentence الخَبَر provides information about the Starting Noun.

Important Note: When Describing words using Adjectives, **both words are Identical** in terms of being defined or undefined and in Parsing الإِعْراب. While in the Nominal Sentence, **the First Noun is defined, and the second word is undefined**. This differentiates the Nominal Sentence from describing words using Adjectives.

Examples for a Nominal Sentence in a Basic Form:

The weather is cold	الجَوُّ بارِدٌ .
The Car is big	السَّيَّارَةُ كَبيرَةٌ .
The tea is hot	الشَّايُ ساخِنٌ .

As you can see, the first word is defined and has Dhamma ـُ ضَمَّة , and the second word is undefined and has Tanween Beddham ـٌ تَنْوين بالضَّم .

Important Note: There is no Verb <u>To be</u> in Arabic.

Now for the next level up, the Predicate الخَبَر can also be a mini sentence. Here are some examples:

3. <u>The Predicate (الخَبَر) as a Preposition or Adverb + a defined Noun</u>

جارّ وَ مَجْرور أو ظَرْف + مُضاف إليه:

I am at home   أَنا في البَيْتِ .

We are on the way   نَحْنُ في الطَّريقِ .

The cat is under the bed   القِطَّةُ تَحْتَ السَّريرِ .

4. <u>The Predicate (الخَبَر) as a Verbal Sentence</u> جُمْلَةٌ فِعْلِيَّة

The boy entered the house   الوَلَدُ دَخَلَ البَيْتَ .

The theatre will start the show   المَسْرَحُ سَيَبْدَأ العَرْضَ .

5. <u>The Predicate (الخَبَر) as a Nominal Sentence</u> جُمْلَةٌ إسْمِيَّة

The lady, her name is Sonia   السَّيِّدَةُ إسْمُها سونْيا .

The singer, his voice is beautiful   المُغَنّي صَوْتُهُ جَميلٌ .

Exercise 9: Practice the difference between Nominal Sentences and describing Nouns using Adjectives. Fill in the missing sections like the examples provided.

Adjective صِفَة	Nominal Sentence جُمْلَةٌ إِسْمِيَّة
شايٌ ساخِنٌ	الشَّايُ ساخِنٌ.
السَّيَّارَةُ الكَبيرَةُ	السَّيَّارَةُ كَبيرَةٌ.
	الجَوُّ بارِدٌ.
وَلَدٌ صَغيرٌ	
	الطَّبيبُ جَيِّدٌ.
قِطَّةٌ جَميلَةٌ	
	الكَلبُ كَبيرٌ.
القَميصُ النَّظيفُ	

Exercise 10: Form Nominal Sentences for these pictures.

Verbal sentences

A Verbal Sentence starts with a **Verb** فِعل . In its simplest form, the Verbal Sentence consists of a **Verb** followed by a **Subject** فاعِل (the doer of the Verb), which can be followed by an **Object** مفْعولٌ بِه .

*Note: Verbs are always in a **Singular Form** in the beginning of a sentence, regardless of the Subject being Singular, Dual or Plural.*

Remember: Verb – Subject – Object

Examples:

قَرَأ آدَمُ الكِتابَ.

كَتَبَتْ مُنى الدَّرْسَ.

يُنيرُ القَمَرُ السَّماءَ.

A great attribute of the Arabic language is that you can shuffle the words in a sentence and begin with any word. You will need to make some minor changes, like adding a Pronoun and changing Vowels according to Parsing, and the meaning will remain the same. The order of words usually means that there's a focus on the first word, and this is part of the Arabic language Eloquence.

<u>So, we can change the order of words in the previous sentences:</u>

قَرَأ آدَمُ الكِتابَ.

آدَمُ قَرَأ الكِتابَ.

الكِتابُ قَرَأهُ آدَمُ.

Exercise 11: Change the words order to create different sentences. Create your own sentences and make the necessary changes.

كَتَبَتْ مُنى الدَّرْسَ.

يُنيرُ القَمَرُ السَّماءَ.

Your sentences:

The relative Adjective النِّسْبَة

To describe the nationality, country, language, etc.: The letter يّ (with a stress ّ) is added to the end of the word for the Masculine, and the letters ة + يّ (with a stress and *Fat7a* َ) is added for the Feminine. If the word ends with an ا or ة , they are omitted and replaced by the يّ or يّة . The letter before يّ will have *Kasra* ِ . See examples:

The Relative Adjective النِّسْبَة

Translation	المُؤَنَّث Feminine	المُذَكَّر Masculine	
Asian	آسْيَوِيَّة	آسْيَوِيّ	آسيا
Australian	أُسْتُرالِيَّة	أُسْتُرالِيّ	أُسْتُرالْيا
African	أَفْريقِيَّة	أَفْريقيّ	أَفْريقْيا
American	أَمْريكِيَّة	أَمْريكِيّ	أَمْريكا
European	أوروبِيَّة	أوروبِيّ	أوروبّا
Egyptian	مِصْريَّة	مِصْريّ	مِصْر
Jordanian	أُرْدُنِيَّة	أُرْدُنِيّ	الأُرْدُن
Sudanese	سودانِيَّة	سودانِيّ	السّودان
British	بريطانِيَّة	بريطانِيّ	بريطانْيا
French	فَرَنْسِيَّة	فَرَنْسِيّ	فَرَنْسا
German	أَلْمانِيَّة	أَلْمانِيّ	أَلْمانْيا
International	دَوْلِيَّة	دَوْلِيّ	دَوْلَة

Global	عالَمِيَّة	عالَمِيّ	عالَم
Arab	عَرَبِيَّة	عَرَبِيّ	
English	إنْجليزِيَّة	إنْجليزيّ	
Foreign	أَجْنَبِيَّة	أَجْنَبِيّ	
Local	مَحَلِّيَّة	مَحَلِّيّ	

Examples:

1. I am from India. So, I am Indian.

أَنا مِن الهِنْد. إذَنْ، أَنا هِنْديَّة.

- إذَن *Means: So. And it is also written* إذًا .

2. He is European because he is from Switzerland.

هُوَ أوروبِيٌّ لِأَنَّهُ مِنْ سويسْرا.

- لِأَنَّ *Means because. It is used In Colloquial, and the word* عَشان *is also used. Any Possessive Pronoun can be added to it:*

لِأَنَّني – لِأَنَّنا – لِأَنَّكَ – لِأَنَّكِ – لِأَنَّكُما – لِأَنَّكُمْ – لِأَنَّكُنَّ – لِأَنَّهُ – لِأَنَّها – لِأَنَّهُما – لِأَنَّهُم – لِأَنَّهُنَّ.

عَشانْ أَنا – عَشانْ إحْنا – عَشانْ إنْتَ – عَشانْ إنْتِ – عَشانْ إنتوا – عَشانْ هُوَّ – عَشانْ هِيَّ – عَشانْ هُمّا

3. You are from Brazil, so, you are Brazilian.

أَنْتَ مِن البَرازيل، إذَنْ أَنْتَ بَرازيليّ.

4. We are from Nigeria, we are Nigerian.

نَحْنُ مِن نَيْجيْريا، نَحْنُ نَيْجيريّون.

5. This is book is written in the English language and translated into Arabic.

هذا الكِتابُ مَكْتوبٌ بِاللُّغَةِ الإنْجليزِيَّةِ وَ مُتَرْجَمٌ إلى العَرَبِيَّة.

6. What is your local currency?

ما هِيَ عُمْلَتُكُمُ المَحَلِّيَّة ؟

7. I want to go to the International Airport.

أُريدُ أَنْ أَذْهَبَ إلى المَطارِ الدَّوْليّ.

- To + any Present Verb in Arabic is expressed by using:

أَنْ + الفِعْلُ المُضارِعُ مَنْصوب : أُريدُ أَنْ أَذْهَبَ – أَنْ أَشْرَبَ – أَنْ أَخْرُجَ – أَنْ أَتَعَلَّمَ

I want to go – to drink – to go out – to learn

Note: In Colloquial Arabic, أَنْ *is not added. So, we just say:*

عايِزْ أَروح – بَدّي أَشْرَب – أُريد اخْرُج – أَبْغى أَتْعَلَّم

These are four different Colloquial alternatives to say I want: The first is Egyptian, the second is levant, and the third and fourth is for the Gulf region.

Exercise 12: Translate the following sentences:

1. I am at the International Airport.

   ----

2. The Japanese currency is the Yen.

   ----

3. We learn the Arabic language because we love it.

   ----

4. There is an Arabic movie at the Cinema.

   ----

5. I went to the local market.

   ----

6. Pakistan is an Asian country.

   ----

7. I would like to drink mineral water.

   ----

8. He is a comedian actor.

Parsing الإعْراب

As you noticed in the previous topics, Vowels at end of words differ according to the word position in a Sentence. The following tables has the basic rules for Grammatical Parsing that you need in this stage.

قَواعِدُ الإعْرابِ النَّحْوِيّ

Words are either in *Raf3* رَفْع , *Nasb* نَصْب , *Jarr* جَرّ , or *Jazm* جَزْم state. The first table shows the different Parsing states of words according to their form and position in a sentence. The second table shows the different Parsing tools used in these states, according to being singular, Dual or Plural, and according to the last letter in the word being a consonant or a vowel.

Different Parsing states of words according to their form and position in a sentence:			
الجَزْم	الجَرّ	النَّصْب	الرَّفْع
الفِعْلُ المُضارِعُ المَسْبوقُ بِأَداةِ جَزْم **The Present Verb** Preceded by certain *Jazm* tools (See examples below).	المُضافُ إلَيْه **The Genitive** The defined Noun following an undefined Noun, or an Adverb.	المَفْعولُ بِه **The Object** The Noun on which the Verb falls in the Verbal Sentence.	المُبْتَدَأ **The Subject** The defined Noun at the beginning of a Nominal Sentence.
	الإسْمُ المَجْرور **The Noun** that comes after a Preposition.	الفِعْلُ المُضارِعُ المَسْبوقُ بِأَداةِ نَصْب **The Present Verb** Preceded by certain *Nasb* tools (See examples below).	الخَبَر **The Predicate** The undefined Noun following the Subject in the Nominal sentence.
			الفاعِل **The Subject** The Doer of the Verb in the Verbal Sentence.
			الفِعْلُ المُضارِع **The Present Tense Verb**

Note: For the Past tense and the Command tense Verbs:

الفِعْلُ الماضي مَبْنِي على الفَتْح، وَ فِعْلُ الأمْرِ مَبْني عَلى السُّكون.

Parsing tools

الجَزْم	الجَرّ	النَّصْب	الرَّفْع
السُّكونُ عَلى آخِرِ حَرْف الفِعْلُ المُضارِعُ صحيحُ الآخِر المُفْرَد المَسْبوق بِأَداة جَزْم أَدَواتُ جَزْمِ الفِعْل: لَمْ – لَمَّا – لامُ الأَمْر – لا النَّاهِيَة إنْ – ما – مَنْ – أَنّى – مَهْما – أَيّ – مَتى – أَيّانَ – أَيْنَ – إذْما – حَيْثُما – كَيْفَما – إذا	الكَسْرَة تَحْتَ آخِرِ حَرْف الإسْمُ المُفْرَد – جَمْعُ التَّكْسير – جَمْعُ المُؤَنَّثِ السَّالِم	الفَتْحَةُ عَلى آخِرِ حَرْف الإسْمُ المُفْرَد – جَمْعُ التَّكْسير الفِعْلُ المُضارِعُ صحيحُ الآخِر وَ مُعْتَلُّ الآخِرِ المَمْنوعُ مِنَ الصَّرْفِ المَسْبوقِ بِأَداةِ نَصْب أَدَواتُ نَصْبِ الفِعْلِ المُضارِع: أَنْ – لَنْ – إذَنْ – كَيْ – لامُ التَّعْليل – لامُ التَّأْكيد – واوُ المَعِيَّة – فاءُ السَّبَبِيَّة – حَتّى – ثُمَّ – أَوْ	الضَّمَّةُ عَلى آخِرِ حَرْف الإسْمُ المُفْرَد – جَمْعُ التَّكْسير جَمْعُ المُؤَنَّثِ السَّالِم الإسْمُ المَمْنوعُ مِنَ الصَّرْف الفِعْلُ المُضارِعُ المُفْرَدُ صحيحُ الآخِر
حَذْفُ حَرْفِ العِلَّة الفِعْلُ المُضارِعُ مُعْتَلُّ الآخِر	الياء الإسْمُ المُثَنّى جَمْعُ المُذَكَّرِ السَّالِم الأَسْماءُ الخَمْسَة : أَب – أَخ – حَم – فو – ذو	الياء الإسْمُ المُثَنّى جَمْعُ المُذَكَّرِ السَّالِم	الأَلِف الإسْمُ المُثَنّى
حَذْفُ النّون الأَفْعالُ الخَمْسَة : يَفْعَلان – تَفْعَلان – يَفْعَلون تَفْعَلون – تَفْعَلين	الفَتْحَة المَمْنوعُ مِنَ الصَّرْف	الأَلِف الأَسْماءُ الخَمْسَة : أَب – أَخ – حَم – فو – ذو	الواو جَمْعُ المُذَكَّرِ السَّالِم الأَسْماءُ الخَمْسَة : أَب – أَخ – حَم – فو – ذو
		حَذْفُ النّون الأَفْعالُ الخَمْسَة: يَفْعَلان – تَفْعَلان – يَفْعَلون تَفْعَلون – تَفْعَلين	ثُبوتُ النّون الأَفْعالُ الخَمْسَة: يَفْعَلان – تَفْعَلان – يَفْعَلون تَفْعَلون – تَفْعَلين
		الكَسْرَة جَمْعُ المُؤَنَّثِ السَّالِم	

Important Note: Some words have a long vowel as their last letter; hence, they will not take any short Vowels. In this case we say in the Parsing الإعْراب that the short vowel is estimated on the end of the word:

مَرْفوعٌ بِالضَّمَّةِ المُقَدَّرَةِ عَلى آخِرِه – مَنْصوبٌ بِالكَسْرَةِ المُقَدَّرَةِ عَلى آخِرِه – مَكْسورٌ بِالكَسْرَةِ المُقَدَّرَةِ عَلى آخِرِه.

Examples:

أَنا – هذا – سَلْوى – رَنا – الصُّغْرى – مُسْتَشْفى – يَخْشى – أَنْسى – أَبو – أَخو – كيلو – مَدْعو – يَعْلو – يَعْفو – يَنْجو – الّذي – الّتي – أَبي – المُحامي – صَديقي

Negation   النَّفْي

Negation tools are used for Nouns, Past and Present tense Verbs, and Nominal and Verbal sentences. When a Negation tool precedes a word, it might affect its parsing الإعْراب , which will affect the last letters of the word: either the short vowel on the last letter will differ, or in the case of Dual and Plural words, the ن will be omitted. (You will find the details in the previous Parsing tools table).

أَدَواتُ النَّفْي Negation Tools			
Usage	مِثال	الاسْتِخْدام	الأَداة
Used for: - Answering with No.	تُريدُ ماء؟ لا ، شُكْرًا.	تُسْتَعْمَل في : - الجَوابُ بِالنَّفْي.	لا
- Negation of Type.	- لا رَجُلَ في البَيْت.	- نَفْيُ الجِنْس. **تَنْصِبُ** الإسْمَ الَّذي يَأْتي بَعْدَها.	
- Negation of Unit.	لا شَيْءٌ عَلى الأَرْض – لا حَليبٌ في السّوق.	- نَفْيُ الوِحْدَة.	
- Negation of Nouns.	لا هذا وَ لا ذلك – لا الوَلَدُ و لا البِنْتُ في البَيْت.	- نَفْيُ الإسْم.	
- Negation of Past tense Verbs.	لا أَكَلَ وَ لا شَرِبَ.	- نَفْيُ الفِعْلِ الماضي.	
- Negation of Present tense verbs.	هُوَ لا يَعْمَلُ في المَساء.	- نَفْيُ الفِعْلِ المُضارِع.	
- Prohibition.	لا تَخْرُجْ في البَرْد.	- **النَّهْي**. وَتَدْخُل على الفِعْلِ المُضارِع **فَتَجْزِمُه.**	

English note	Example	Explanation	
- Present tense Verbs	لَمْ تَأْكُلْ البِنْتُ الطَّعام.	تَدْخُل على الفِعْلِ المُضارِع **فَتَجْزِمُه** و تَقْلِبُهُ مِنَ الزَّمَنِ المُضارِعِ إلى الزَّمَنِ الماضي.	لَمْ
- Present tense Verbs.	حَضَرَ المُدَرِّس وَ لَمّا يَحْضُرْ الطّالِب. حَضَرِ المُدَرِّس (و ماحَضَرْش/ ما حَضَر) الطّالِب.	تَدْخُلُ عَلى الفِعْلِ المُضارِع **فَتَجْزِمُهُ** وَ تَنْفي وُقوعَ الفِعْلِ في الزَّمَنِ الماضي المُسْتَمِرّ.	لَمّا
- Nouns. - Past and Present tense Verbs.	ما طارِقٌ إلّا فاعِلُ خَيْر – ما هذا بِجَديد. ما حَضَرَ أَحَد – ما أقولُ إلّا الحَقّ. ما حَضَرْش حَدّ / ما حَضَر أحَد/حَدا.	<u>تُسْتَخْدَمُ في:</u> - نَفْيُ الأَسْماء. - نَفْيُ الفِعْلِ الماضي وَ الفِعْلِ المُضارِع.	ما
- Present tense Verbs.	لَنْ أَذْهَبَ اليَوْمَ إلى العَمَل. مِش هروح الشُّغْل اليوم / ما راحَ أروح الشُّغْل اليوم.	تَدْخُلُ على الفِعْلِ المُضارِع **فَتَنْصُبه** وَ تَنْفي وُقوعَ الفِعْلِ في زَمَنِ المُسْتَقْبَل.	لَنْ مِشْ – ما
- Nouns.	لَيْسَ لَكَ هذا. لَيْسَ الوَقْتُ مناسِبًا. ده مِش ليك / الوَقْت مو مناسِب.	تَدْخُلُ عَلى الإسْم. وتَدْخُلُ عَلى الجُمْلَةِ الإسْمِيةِ فَتَرْفَعُ المُبْتَدَأ وَ **تَنْصِبُ** الخَبَر.	لَيْسَ مِشْ – مو
- Nouns.	الباب غَيْرُ مَفْتوحٍ. الباب (مِش / مو) مَفْتوح.	تَدْخُل على الجُمْلَةِ الإسْمِيَّة. و تُعْرَبُ حَسَبَ مَوْقِعِها مِنَ الجُمْلَةِ. وَ هِيَ مُضافٌ و ما بعدَها مُضافٌ إلَيْه.	غَيْر مِشْ – مو
- Past and Present tense Verbs.	إنْ أُريدُ إلّا الإصْلاح.	تَدْخُلُ على الفِعْلِ الماضي وَ الفِعْلِ المُضارِع.	إنْ

Exercise 13: Choose the correct Negation tool from the brackets.

(لَمْ – لَنْ – لَيْسَ) هذا الذي أُريدُه.

(لَمْ – ما – غَيْر) أَذْهَبُ إلى الدَّرس.

أُريدُ قَميصًا (لا – ما – غَيْرَ) هذا .

(لَنْ – ما – لَمّا) أَخْرُجَ اليَوْم.

(لَم – ما – لَيْسَ) فَهِمتُ الكَلام.

المَحَلُّ (لَنْ – ما – غَيْرُ) مَفْتوح.

(ما – غَيْرَ – لَا) تَسْأَلْني عَن السَّبَب.

(لَنْ – لا – ما) أنا إلّا رَسول.

(لَيْسَ – لَنْ – ما) تُصَدِّقَ ما حَدَث!

(لَم – ما – لا) طَعامٌ في البَيْت.

Numbers   الأَرْقام

When studying Arabic Numbers, it is worth mentioning that the shape of today's Western Numerals was invented by the Arab Mathematician Al-Khwarezmi (AD780-850), who is also considered the father of Algebra (from the Arabic word جَبْر which means forcing). The name Al-Khwarezmi also led to the term "Algorithm" (Through Latin: Algoritmi)

Al-Khwarezmi shaped the Numerals based on the Number of Angles:

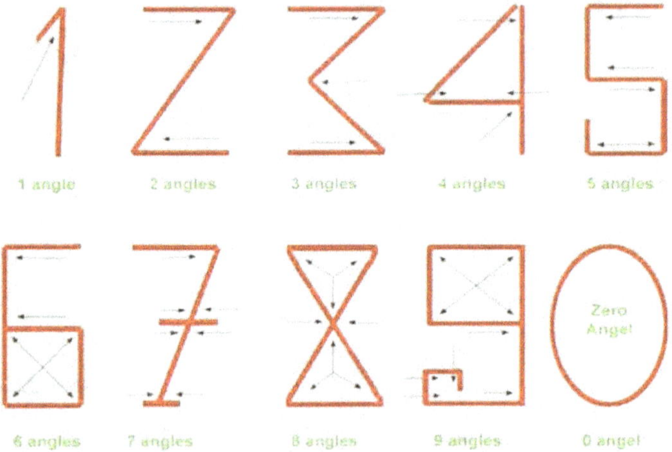

However, Arabic Numerals now look different, and most probably they come from Indian Numerals. Now let us learn the Arabic Numbers:

Transliteration	الرَّقَم	الرَّقم	Numeral
Sefr	صِفْر	٠	0
Wa7ed	واحِد	١	1
Ethnan	إثْنان	٢	2
Thalatha	ثَلاثَة	٣	3
Arba3a	أَرْبَعَة	٤	4
Khamsa	خَمْسَة	٥	5
Setta	سِتَّة	٦	6
Sab3a	سَبْعَة	٧	7
Thamaneya	ثَمانِية	٨	8
Tes3a	تِسْعَة	٩	9
3ashra	عَشْرَة	١٠	10

Note: *There is hardly any difference between the Classical and the Colloquial version of these Arabic Numerals.*

Colloquial Arabic	Classical Arabic	العَدَد	Number
حِداشْر – إحْدَعَش	أَحَدَ عَشَرَ إحْدى عَشْرَةَ	١١	11
إتناشَر – إتْنَعَش	إثْنا عَشَرَ إثْنَتا عَشْرَةَ	١٢	12
تَلَتاشَر – تَلَتَّعَش	ثَلاثَ عَشْرَةَ ثَلاثَةَ عَشَرَ	١٣	13
أَرْبَعْتاشَر – أَرْبَعْتَعَش	أَرْبَعَ عَشْرَةَ أَرْبَعَةَ عَشَرَ	١٤	14
خَمَسْتاشَر – خَمَسْتَعَش	خَمْسَ عَشْرَةَ خَمْسَةَ عَشَرَ	١٥	15
سِتّاشَر – سِتَّعَش	سِتَّ عَشْرَةَ سِتَّةَ عَشَرَ	١٦	16
سَبَعْتاشَر – سَبَعْتَعَش	سَبْعَ عَشْرَةَ سَبْعَةَ عَشَرَ	١٧	17
تَمَنْتاشَر – تَمَنْتَعَش	ثَمانيَ عَشْرَةَ ثَمانِيَةَ عَشَرَ	١٨	18
تِسَعْتاشَر – تِسَعْتَعَش	تِسْعَ عَشْرَةَ تِسْعَةَ عَشَرَ	١٩	19
عِشْرين	عِشْرون	٢٠	20

Note: The difference between the first and the second version of the classical Arabic version of numbers is due to Grammatical rules corresponding to the counted object. This will be explained shortly.

Colloquial Arabic	Classical Arabic	العَدَد	Number
عِشْرين	عِشْرون	٢٠	20
تَلاتين	ثَلاثون	٣٠	30
أَرْبعين	أَرْبَعون	٤٠	40
خَمْسين	خَمْسون	٥٠	50
سِتّين	سِتّون	٦٠	60
سَبْعين	سَبْعون	٧٠	70
تَمانين	ثَمانون	٨٠	80
تِسْعين	تِسْعون	٩٠	90
مِيّة	مائة/مِئة	١٠٠	100

Note: مائة / مِئة is *pronounced* the same but written in two different ways.

Colloquial Arabic	Classical Arabic	Number
مِيّة	مائة/مِئة	Hundred
أَلْف	أَلْف	Thousand
مِلْيون	مِلْيون	Million
مِلْيار	مِلْيار	Billion

The Complete table of Numbers:

مِئَة مِيّه	100	واحِدٌ وَعِشرون وَاحِد وِ عِشرين	21	أَحَدَ عَشَر حِداشَر – حِدَعَش	11	واحِد	1
مِئَتان مِيتين	200	إِثنانِ وَعِشرون اتْنين وِ عِشرين	22	إِثْنى عَشَر اِتْناشَر – اِتْنَعَش	12	إِثْنان اِثْنين – اِثْنين	2
ثَلاثُمِئَة تُلْتُمِيّه – تَلاتْمِيّه	300	ثَلاثَةٌ وَعِشرون تَلاتَه وِ عِشرين	23	ثَلاثَةَ عَشَر تلتّاشَر – تَلتَّعَش	13	ثَلاثَة تَلاتَه	3
أَرْبَعُمِئَة رُبْعُمِيّه – أَرْبَعْمِيّه	400	أَرْبَعَةٌ وَعِشرون أَرْبَعَه وِ عِشرين	24	أَرْبَعَةَ عَشَر أَرْبَعْتاشَر – أَرْبَعْتَعَش	14	أَرْبَعَة	4
خَمْسُمِئَة خُمْسُمِيّه – خَمَسْمِيّة	500	خَمْسَةٌ وَعِشرون خَمْسَه وِ عِشرين	25	خَمْسَةَ عَشَر خَمْسْتاشَر – خَمَسْتَعَش	15	خَمْسَة	5
سِتُّمِئَة سُتُّمِيّه – سِتُّمِيّه	600	سِتَّةٌ وَعِشرون سِتَّه وِ عِشرين	26	سِتَّةَ عَشَر سِتّاشَر – سِتَّعَش	16	سِتَّة	6
سَبْعُمِئَة سُبْعُمِيّه – سَبِعْمِيّه	700	سَبْعَةٌ وَعِشرون سَبْعَه وِ عِشرين	27	سَبْعَةَ عَشَر سَبْعْتاشَر – سَبْعْتَعَش	17	سَبْعَة	7
ثَمانُمِئَة تُمْنُمِيّه – تَمانْمِيّه	800	ثَمانِيَةٌ وَعِشرون تَمانْيَه وِ عِشرين	28	ثَمانِيَةَ عَشَر تَمانْتاشَر – تَمْنْتَعَش	18	ثَمانِية	8
تِسْعُمِئَة تُسْعُمِيّه – تِسِعْمِيّه	900	تِسْعَةٌ وَعِشرون تِسْعَه وِ عِشرين	29	تِسْعَةَ عَشَر تِسْعْتاشَر – تِسْعْتَعَش	19	تِسْعَة	9
أَلْف	1000	ثَلاثون تَلاتين	30	عِشرون عِشرين	20	عَشْرَة	10
مِلْيون	Million	أَرْبَعون أَرْبَعين	40				
مِلْيار	Billion	خَمْسون خَمْسين	50				

		سِتُّون سِتِّين	60			
		سَبْعون سَبْعين	70			
		ثَمانون تَمانين	80			
		تِسْعون تِسْعين	90			

Note: Words in Grey are the Colloquial form. The first is the Egyptian dialect, and the second is the Levant / Gulf area dialect.

The following rules are important Grammatical rules. They are not observed in the Colloquial form.

- Number **one and two** <u>always agree with the Counted Noun in Gender and Diacritical marks</u> (عَلامَاتُ التَّشْكِيل), as the number come after the Noun and is treated as an Adjective:

حَضَرَ رَجُلٌ واحِدٌ – حَضَرَت امْرَأَةٌ واحِدَةٌ – حَضَرَ رَجُلانِ وَ امْرَأَتانِ

قابَلْتُ رَجُلًا واحِدًا – قابَلْتُ امْرَأَةً واحِدَةً – قابَلْتُ رَجُلَيْنِ وَامرَأَتَيْنِ

Note: The Counted Noun امْرَأَة / رَجُل in Single and Dual Forms in the first line examples are a Subject فاعِل. And in the second line examples are an Object مَفْعولٌ بِه. This is because قابَلْتُ (meaning: I met) consists of : تُ + قابَلَ. This is a Verb: قابَلَ and a Subject: تُ

- Number **Two** is Grammatically treated as the Dual Noun:

حَضَرَ رَجُلانِ – حَضَرَتْ امْرَأَتانِ

قابَلْتُ رَجُلَيْنِ – قابَلْتُ امْرَأَتَيْنِ

- Numbers from **3 to 10** always <u>contradict the Counted Noun in Gender</u>, so it is Masculine with the Feminine Noun, and Feminine with the Masculine Noun. The Diacritical marks (عَلامَاتُ التَّشْكِيل) of the Number here depends on its position in the sentence:

حَضَرَ أَرْبَعَةُ عُمّالٍ – حَضَرَتْ أَرْبَعُ عامِلاتٍ

قابَلْتُ عامِلَيْنِ – قابَلْتُ أَرْبَعَ عامِلاتٍ

The counted Noun **here is treated as** مُضافٌ إلَيْهِ مَجْرورٌ بالكَسْرَة

This rule of opposite Gender applies also in the Combination Numbers, i.e., Twenty-Four, Thirty-Nine, etc.:

أَرْبَعٌ وَ عِشْرونَ ساعَةً – تِسْعَةٌ وَ ثَلاثونَ قَلَمًا

- Number **11** and **12** <u>agree with the</u> Counted Noun <u>Gender</u> in both parts:

  Number **11**:
  - Is always   مَبْنِي عَلَى الفَتْح   in both Parts.

  حَضَرَ أَحَدَ عَشَرَ رَجُلاً – حَضَرَتْ إحْدى عَشْرَةَ امْرَأَةً

  قابَلْتُ أَحَدَ عَشَرَ رَجُلاً – قابَلْتُ إحْدى عَشْرَةَ امْرَأَةً

  Number **12**:
  - The first part is treated like the Dual Noun
    يُرْفَعُ بِالأَلِف، وَيُنْصَبُ وَ يُجَرُّ بِالياء و حَذْفِ النّون.

  - The second part عَشَرَ remains always with *Fat7a* مَبْنِي عَلَى الفَتْح

  حَضَرَ إثْنا عَشَرَ رَجُلاً – حَضَرَتْ إثْنَتَا عَشْرَةَ امْرَأَةً

  قابَلْتُ إثْنَيْ عَشَرَ رَجُلاً – قابَلْتُ إثْنَتَي عَشْرَةَ امْرَأَةً

The Counted Noun **here is treated as** تَمْييز مَبْني عَلَى الفَتْح

- Numbers **13 to 19** <u>contradict the</u> Counted Noun <u>Gender</u> in its first part and <u>follow it in the second part</u>. It is always مَبْني عَلَى الفَتْح in both parts:

  حَضَرَ خَمْسَةَ عَشَرَ رَجُلاً – حَضَرَت ثَلاثَ عَشْرَةَ امْرَأَةً

  قابَلْتُ سِتَّةَ عَشَرَ رَجُلاً – قابَلْتُ تِسْعَ عَشْرَةَ امْرَأَةً

- **Twenty, Thirty, Forty, ...to Ninety (أَلْفاظُ العُقود):** Always follow the same rule as
  جَمْعُ المُذَكَّرِ السَّالِم. تُرْفَعُ بِالواو وَ تُنْصَبُ وَتُجَرُّ بِالياء:

  حَضَرَ عِشْرونَ رَجُلاً – حَضَرَتْ ثَمانونَ امْرَأَةً

  قابَلْتُ ثَلاثينَ رَجُلًا – قابَلْتُ خَمْسينَ امْرَأَةً

- **Hundred(s) and Thousand(s):** أَلْف – مائَة

    - The number connected to the word مائَة is always Masculine, while the number connected to the word أَلْف is always Feminine.

أَرْبَعُمائَة – تِسْعُمائَة

أَرْبَعَةُ آلافٍ – تِسْعَةُ آلافٍ

    - The Diacritical Marks (عَلاماتُ التَّشْكيل) for these numbers depend on their position in a sentence:

تُرْفَع بِالضَّمَّةِ لِلمُفْرَدِ وَ الجَمْعِ، وبِالأَلِفِ لِلْمُثَنَّى. و تُنْصَب بِالفَتْحَة لِلمُفْرد و الجَمْع، و بِالياء لِلمُثَنَّى. وَ تُجَرّ بِالكَسْرَة لِلمُفْرَد و الجَمع ، و بِالياء لِلْمُثَنَّى:

حَضَرَ مِئَّةُ رَجُلٍ – قابَلْتُ مائَة امْرَأَةٍ

حَضَرَ أَلْفُ رَجُلٍ – قابَلْتُ أَلْفَي امْرَأَةٍ

حَضَرَ مائَتَا رَجُلٍ – قابَلْتُ مائَتَي امْرَأَةٍ

حَضَرَ أَلْفا رَجُلٍ – قابَلْتُ أَلْفَي امْرَأَةٍ

حَضَرَ خَمْسُمائَةُ رَجُلٍ – قابَلْتُ خَمْسُمائَة امْرَأَةٍ

حَضَرَ خَمْسَةُ آلافٍ طالِبٍ – قابَلْتُ خَمْسَةَ آلافٍ طالِبَةٍ

The Counted Noun   : الإسْمُ المَعْدود

- Numbers **3 to 10**: The Counted Noun is Plural *Majroor* جَمْع مَجْرور
- Numbers **11 to 99**: The Counted Noun is Singular *Mansoob* مُفْرَد مَنْصوب
- Number **100** and its **multiples**: The Counted Noun is Singular *Majroor* مُفْرَد مَجْرور

Exercise 14: Translate the following:

17 cats   20 books   11 players   400 students

----

5 pens   16 men   7 days   24 hours

I sleep 8 hours a day, and I work 5 days a week.

There are 365 days in a year.

الحافِلَةُ تَصِلُ السَّاعَةَ السَّابِعَةَ صَباحًا. (الباص يِوْصَل السّاعَه سَبْعَه الصُّبْح)

إِبْنَتي عُمْرُها خَمْسُ سَنَوات. (بِنْتي عُمْرَها خَمَسْ سِنين)

أَخي في أَمْريكا مُنْذُ عَشْرِ أَعْوام. (أَخويا في أَمْريكا مِن عَشَرْ سِنين)

بَنى أَبي هذا البَيْتَ سَنَةَ أَلْفٍ و تُسْعُمائَةٍ و سَبْعين. (أَبويا بَنى البيت دا سَنة أَلْف و تُسْعُمِيَّه و سَبْعين)

Time الوَقْت

This is the Vocabulary you need to converse about the time in Arabic:

The Time	الوَقْت
The clock	السَّاعَة
Appointment	مَوْعِد
Now	الآن
Hour	ساعَة
Minute **Singular** Minutes **Plural**	دَقيقَة دَقائِق
Second **Singular** Seconds **Plural**	ثانِيَة ثَواني
Quarter	رُبْع
Third	ثُلْث تِلْت
Half	نِصْف نُصّ
How many?	كَمْ؟
What is the time?	كَم السَّاعَة؟ السّاعَه كام؟
Morning time. AM	صَباحًا
Evening time. PM	مَساءً
Exactly/Sharp	تَمامًا
About/Roughly	تَقْريبًا
Except for	إلّا

The Dawn	الفَجْر
Morning-time	الصُّبْح
The Noon	الظُّهْر
The Afternoon	العَصْر
The Sunset/Dusk	المَغْرِب
Night-time	اللَّيْل

Important Notes:

- When saying the time, Numbers follow the Form الفاعِلَة . So, we say:

الواحِدة – الثّانِيَة – الثّالِثَة – الرّابِعَة – الخامِسَة – السّادِسَة – السّابِعَة – الثّامِنَة – التّاسِعَة – العاشِرَة – الحادِيَة عَشْرَة – الثّانِيَة عَشْرَة

And these are said after the Word السّاعَة or السّاعَةُ الآن (According to the context of the sentence). So, we say:

السّاعَةُ الآنَ الواحِدَةَ تَمامًا – في السّاعَةِ الحادِيَةِ عَشْرَة صَباحًا – في السّاعَةِ السّابِعَةِ مَساءً

- The Short vowel on the *Taa Marboota* ة for the number expressing the time will be identical to the word السّاعَة as it is an **Adjective** for it. Therefore, it will depend on the position of the word السّاعَة) i.e. Subject, Object, Genitive, etc.).

Note: *In Colloquial Arabic however, this doesn't apply as the Time is said in its basic Number Form (and the Taa Marboota ة is pronounced as a Ha ه) :*

السّاعَه وَحْده – السّاعَه اتنين – السّاعه تلاته – السّاعَه أَرْبَعَه – السّاعَه خَمْسَه – السّاعَه سِته – السّاعَه سَبْعَه – السّاعَه تَمانْيه – السّاعَه تِسْعَه – السّاعَه عَشْرَه – السّاعَه حِداشَر / حِدَعش – السّاعَه اتْناشَر / اتْنعَش.

- When saying the Time in Classical Arabic, the Grammatical Rules of Numbers mentioned in the Numbers Section will apply. So, the number will contradict the counted Noun where this applies. For example:

1. We say خَمْسُ دقائِقَ, because دَقائِقَ is a Feminine word (Plural of a Feminine Noun دَقيقَة). The word دَقائِقَ Always come with Fat7a َة.

2. We also say ثَلاثٌ وَ عِشْرونَ دَقيقَة

Note: *In Colloquial Arabic these rules are not observed. So, we say:*

السّاعَه خَمْسَه و عَشْرَه – السّاعَه حْداشَر الصُّبح – السّاعَه سَبْعَه اَلّا رُبْع – السّاعَه اتنين و نُص إِلّا خَمْسَه – السّاعَه عَشْرَه مَساءً / بِللّيل – السّاعَه تَمانْيه وْ تِلْت – السّاعَه تَلاتَه وِ اتْناشَر دِئيئَه – السّاعَه وَحْده و تَمانْيه و خَمْسين دِئيئَه.

Exercise 15: Translate the Times in the table into Arabic (see examples).

12:00PM	15:20	1:00AM
		الواحِدَةُ صَباحًا وَحْده الصُّبْح
5:10AM	**14:25**	**3:30PM**
	الثانِيَةُ وَ خَمْسٌ وَ عِشرون دَقيقَة إِتْنين وِ خَمْسَه وْ عِشْرين دِئِيئَه/ Dagiga	
04:05	**18:00**	**09:52**
الرَّابِعَةُ وَ خَمْسُ دَقائِقَ صَباحًا أَرْبَعَه وْ خَمْسَه		
Roughly Sunset time	**In the Afternoon time**	**At night**
	وَقْتُ العَصْر	بالليل بِللّيل
The appointment is at 10 in the evening	**Before Dawn**	**At Sunset time**
At 7 o'clock sharp	**Now it's five o'clock**	**The appointment is at 11 in the morning**
		المَوْعِدُ في السّاعَةِ الحادِيَة عَشْرَةَ صَباحًا المَوْعِد السّاعَه خداشَر الصُّبْح

Exercise 16: Word Search puzzle.

Locate the words in the grids and cross them out, then form a word with the remaining letters.

Word search 1:

ر	ي	ف	ت	ق	و
ب	ل	س	ف	ص	ن
ع	ر	ا	ص		ت
إ	أ	ع	ب	م	م
لّا		ة	ا	و	ا
ق	ك	ا	ح	ع	م
ا	م	م	ا	د	ا

<u>**Words to find:**</u>

Hour	Except for	Sharp	Time	How many
In	Quarter	Appointment	Morning	Half

The missing word: -----------------------------------

Word search 2:

ا	ة	ي	ن	ا	ث	ت
م	ف	ص	ن	س	د	ق
س	ة	ت	س	ق	ث	ر
ا	م	ك	ي	ل	ل	ي
ء		ق	ة	ا	ث	ب
ع	ة	ة	س	م	خ	ا

<u>Words to find:</u>

How many	Third	Evening	Five	Second
Minute	Half	About	Six	

The missing word: --------------------------------------

Days of the week أَيَّامُ الأُسْبوع

These are the days of the week and useful Vocabulary for time and date:

The day	أَيَّامُ الأُسْبوع
Saturday	السَّبْت
Sunday	الأَحَد
Monday	الإِثْنَيْن
Tuesday	الثُّلَاثاء
Wednesday	الأَرْبِعاء
Thursday	الخَميس
Friday	الجُمْعَة

Useful Vocabulary

Day	يَوْم
Week	أُسْبوع
Month	شَهْر
Year	عام / سَنَة
Weekend	عُطْلَةُ نِهايَةِ الأُسْبوع
Holiday	عُطْلَة / أَجازَة
Date	تاريخ
Calendar	تَقْويم
Gregorian date	التّاريخُ الميلادي
Hijri (Arabic) date	التّاريخُ الهِجْري

As you now have a wide variety of Arabic Vocabulary, you are now ready to ask questions and give answers. Here are the Arabic Question Tools:

Question tool	مِثال	أَداة الاسْتِفْهام Colloquial العامِيَّة	أَداة الاسْتِفْهام Classical الفُصْحى
Yes or No questions	أَهُوَ الطَّبيبُ المَشْهور؟ Is he the famous doctor?		أَ
Do/Does/Did? **Yes or No** questions	هَلْ تَعْرِف هذِه السَّيِّدَة؟ Do you know this lady?		هَلْ؟
Who?	مَنْ بِالباب؟ Who is at the door?	مين — مِنو	مَنْ؟
What? For Nouns	ما إسْمُك؟ What is your name?	إيه — إيش — شو	ما؟
What? For Verbs	ماذا تَفْعَلين؟ What are you doing?	إيه — إيش — شو	ماذا؟
Why?	لِماذا لا تَأْخُذُ الدَّواء؟ Why are you not taking the medicine?	ليه — ليش	لِمَ - لِماذا؟
Where?	أَيْنَ سَتَذْهَبُ هذا المَساء؟ Where are you going this evening?	فين — وين	أَيْنَ؟
How?	كَيْفَ حالُك؟ How are you doing?	إزّاي — كيف	كَيْفَ؟

English	Example	Colloquial	Question word
How many? People, objects, and time.	كَمْ طالِبًا في الفَصْل؟ How many students in the class? كَم السّاعَةُ الآن؟ What is the time now?	كام	كَمْ ؟
How much? Asking about the price	بِكَم تَذْكَرَةُ القِطار؟ How much is the train ticket?	بِكام	بِكَمْ ؟
Which?	أيُّ لَوْنٍ تُحِبّين؟ Which colour do you like?		أَيّ ؟
When?	مَتى يَبْدَأُ الفيلم؟ When does the film start?	إِمْتى – مِتى	مَتى ؟

Exercise 17: Insert the correct Question tool in the space. You can use more than one if possible.

ـــــــــــــــــ قِطَّةً عِنْدَكَ في البَيْت ؟

ـــــــــــــــــ سَتَذْهَبُ إلى الدَّرْس؟

ـــــــــــــــــ تُريدُ مِن المُدَرِّس ؟

ـــــــــــــــــ سَمِعْتُم الخَبَر؟

ـــــــــــــــــ الرَّجُلُ الّذي في السَّيّارة؟

ـــــــــــــــــ سَيَفْتَحُ المَحَلّ؟

ـــــــــــــــــ البَيْت؟

ـــــــــــــــــ حَقيبةٍ (شَنْطة) تُحِبّين؟

-------------- كيلو البُرْتُقال؟

-------------- أَنْتَ غَضْبان؟

-------------- تَعْمَلُ يَوْمَ الجُمْعَة؟

-------------- تاريخُ ميلادِك؟

Practice writing the previous sentences.

<h1 style="text-align:center">Food and beverages   الطَّعامُ وَ الشَّراب</h1>

Food and beverages are an important part of any culture. The Arab world is full of a large variety of food that is very popular worldwide. In this section, we will study important vocabulary for food and beverages including some famous Arabic ones, and how to order in a restaurant.

<h2 style="text-align:center">Breakfast: الفِطار الإفْطار</h2>

Beverages   المَشْروبات

Water	Milk	Laban	Juice
ماء مَيّا - مَي	حَليب	لَبَن	عَصير

Red Tea	Green Tea	Coffee	Hot chocolate
شاي أَحْمَر	شاي أَخْضَر	قَهْوَة	شوكولاتة ساخِنَة سُخْنَة

Eggs	Foul (type of beans)	Falafel / Ta3meya	Cheese
بَيْض بيض	فول	فَلافِل / طَعْمِيَّة	جُبْنَة جِبْنَه

Bread	Pastries	Feteer (Pastry)	Cake
خُبْز عيش	مُعَجَّنات	فِطير	كيك

Honey	Jam	Yogurt	Tahini
عَسَل	مُرَبّى مِرَبّى	زَبادِي	طَحينَة

Butter	Oil	Vinegar	Spices
زُبْدَة زِبْدَه	زَيْت زيت	خَلّ	تَوابِل

Salt	Black Pepper	Sugar	Sweetener
مِلْح مَلْح	فِلْفِل أَسْوَد	سُكَّر	مُحَلِّي صِناعي

Table	Fork, knife and spoon	Plate	Tissue/Napkin
طاوِلَة طاوْلَه – تَرابيزَه	مِلْعَقَة مَعْلَأَه وَ سِكِّينَة و شوكَة	طَبق طَبَأ	مَنْديل وَرَقيّ مَنْديل وَرَأ

Lunch and Dinner: الغَداء الغَدا وَ العَشاء العَشا

Salad	Soup	Rice	Pasta
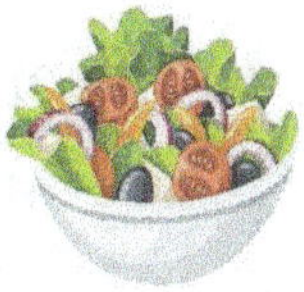	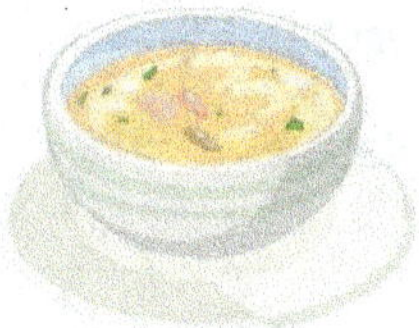	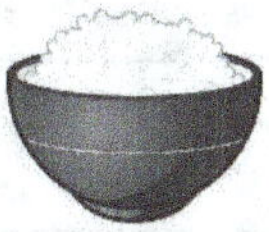	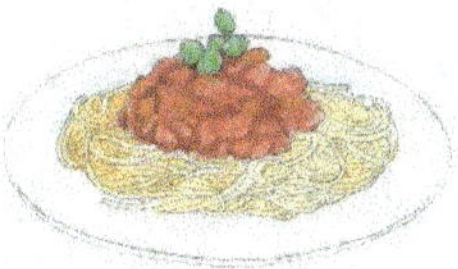
سَلَطَة	شوربَة	رُزّ	مَكَرونَة

Sea food	Fish	Shrimps	Crab
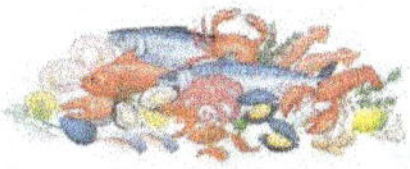	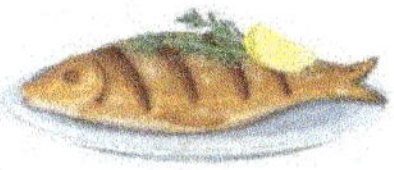	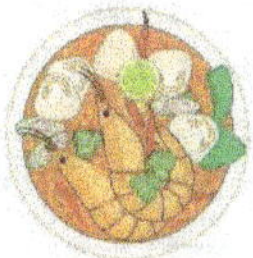	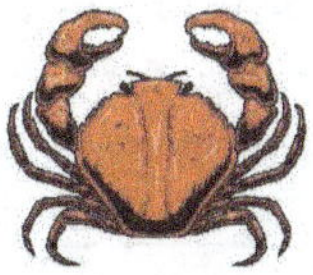
مَأكولات بَحرِيَّة	سَمَك	جَمْبَري	كابوريا

Chicken	Beef	Mutton	Vegetables
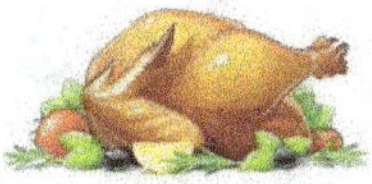	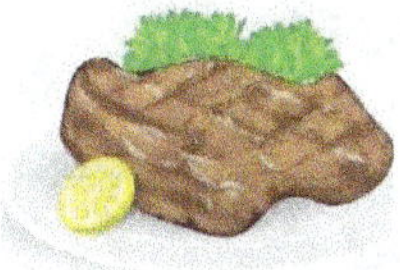	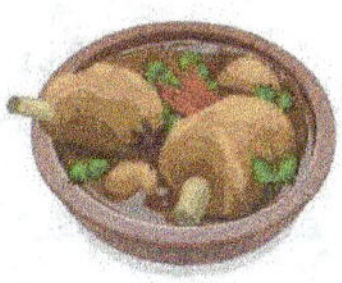	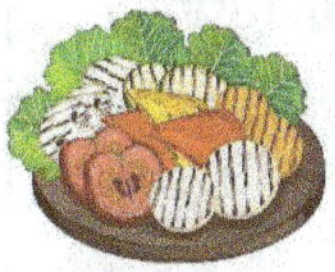
دَجاج فِراخ	لَحم بَقَري	لَحم غَنَم	خُضار

Useful vocabulary for food and beverages

Sweet	حُلْو	Restaurant	مَطْعَم
Sour	حادِق	Waiter Waitress	نادِل جَرْسون نادِلَة جَرْسونه
Hot (spicy)	حَرّاق	Food menu	قائِمَةُ الطَّعام مينْيو
Do you have?	عِنْدَك – عِنْدَكُم	Food	مَأْكولات أَكْل
I want M-F	أُريد عايِز – عايْزَه	Beverages	مَشْروبات شُرْب
How much?	بِكَم؟ بِكام	Meal	وَجْبَة
I bring I bring for you M - F	أَجيب أَجيبَلَك – أَجيبْلِك	Appetizers	مُقَبِّلات
Home delivery	تَوْصيل لِلْبيت	Main meal	الوَجْبَة الأَساسِيَّة
Takeaway	Takeaway	Dessert	حَلَوِيّات
For free	مَجّانًا	Vegetarian	نَباتي
The bill	الفاتورَة - الحِساب	Fresh	طازَج طازَه
Payment	الدَّفْع	Chilled	بارِد
Remaining money	الباقي	Frozen	مُثَلَّج مِتَلِّج
Tip	بَقْشيش	Hot	ساخِن سُخْن
		Boiled	مَسْلوق
		Grilled	مَشْوي
		Fried	مَقْلي

Exercise 18: Connect each word with its translation.

Soup	حَليب
Shrimps	ماء
Beef	عَصير
Milk	جَمْبَري
Water	شوْرْبَة
Juice	لَحْم بَقَري

Coffee	مِلْح
Chicken	كيك
Salad	دَجاج
Salt	سَلَطة
Cake	مَكَرونة
Pasta	قَهْوَة

Eggs	جُبْنَة
Honey	شاي
Pepper	بَيْض
Fish	عَسَل
Cheese	فِلْفِل
Tea	سَمَك

Now that you know all the necessary Vocabulary, let us practice ordering food at a restaurant. The conversations are written in Modern Classical Arabic closest to Colloquial Arabic which is understood in any Arab country. Therefore, you will find some minor changes in short vowels. Colloquial alternatives for some Classical words are written in Grey.

Conversation 1: At the restaurant

في المَطْعَم

النّادِل (الجَرْسون): صَباحِ الخير. تَطْلُبين شيء؟

الزُّبونَة: نَعَم، وَجْبَة إفْطار كامِلَة. و البيض أومْليت بِالْخُضار و الجبْنة مِنْ فَضْلِك.

النّادِل: حاضِر. تَشْرَبين قَهْوَة أو شاي؟

الزُّبونَة: أَشْرَب قَهْوَة مِنْ فَضْلِك، لكِن بَعْدِ الأَكْل.

النّادِل : تَمام.

الزُّبونَة: شُكْرًا.

النّادِل : العَفْو.

Conversation 2: At the seafood restaurant

في مَطْعَمِ المَأْكولاتِ البَحَرِيَّة

الزُّبون: مُمْكِن أَطْلُب الآن لَوْ سَمَحْتِ؟

النّادِلَة (الجَرْسونَه) : طَبْعًا ، تَفَضَّل. إِتْفَضَّل.

الزُّبون : عِنْدَكُم سَمَك طازَج؟ طازَه؟

النّادِلَة: نَعَم (أَيْوه) أَكيد موجود. وَ مُمْكِن تَخْتار بِنَفْسِك مِنَ الثَّلاجَة.

الزُّبون: مُمْتاز! كَمْ سِعْر الكيلو؟

النّادِلَة: حَسَب نَوْع (نوع) السَّمك . السِّعْر يَبْدَأ مِن عِشرين رِيال حَتّى خَمْسين رِيال. وَ عِنْدَنا عَرْض: إذا طَلَبْت سَمَك بِخَمْسين رِيال تَأْخُذ (تاخُد) سَلَطَة مَجّانًا.

الزُّبون: عَظيم جِدًّا ! آخُذ رُزّ وَ بَطاطِس مُحَمَّرَة مَعَ السَّمَك مِنْ فَضْلِك.

النّادِلَة: تَمام. تُحِبُّ أَنْ تَشْرَب عَصير؟ تِحِبّ تِشْرَب عَصير؟

الزُّبون: نَعَم أَيْوَه عَصير لَيْمون سُكَّر خَفيف مِنْ فَضْلِك.

النّادِلَة : حاضِر.

بَعْد الوَجْبَة

النّادِلَة: كُلُّه تَمام؟ All is alright?

الزُّبون : نَعَم ! الأَكْل مُمْتاز، شُكْرًا. مُمْكِن الحِساب؟

النّادِلَة : عَظيم، حاضِر خَمَسْن دقائق وَ أَجيبْلَك الفاتورة.

الزُّبون: شُكْرًا.

Writing a Paragraph

Now let's move onto a great step in this book and start writing our first Paragraph. Read the following paragraph and fill in the table below with the suitable words from it. Write the Parsing الإعْراب for each word.

أنا مَنال. طالِبَةٌ في الجامِعَةِ في السَّنَةِ الأولى، و أَدْرُسُ الطِّبَّ حَتّى أَعْمَلَ طَبيبَةَ قَلْب. عِنْدي أَخٌ وأُخْت. أَخي يُحِبُّ الرِّياضَة - خاصَّةً السِّباحَة - وَأُخْتي تَعْمَلُ (تِشْتَغَل) مُدَرِّسَة.

أنا أَسْكُنُ في لَنْدَنْ. يَومي يَبْدَأُ مِنَ السّاعَةِ السّابِعَةِ صَباحًا (السّاعَه سَبَعَه الصُّبْح). أَتَناوَلُ الفُطورَ (أَفْطَر) ثُمَّ آخُذُ الحافِلَةَ (الباص) إلى الجامِعَةِ، وأَرْجِعُ في الخامِسَةِ (أَرْجَع السّاعَه خَمْسَه) تَقْريبًا. وَأَنْت؟

Defined Nouns	Undefined Nouns	Prepositions / Conjunctions	Pronouns	Verbs

Exercise 19: Compose a similar Paragraph about yourself, and then fill in the table below with your words and the correct Parsing.

Defined Nouns	Undefined Nouns	Prepositions / Conjunctions	Pronouns	Verbs

Congratulations! You have now covered what you need to be able to read, write and speak well in Arabic in both the Classical and Colloquial forms. You can now express yourself using sound sentences, with Nouns, Verbs, Pronouns, Prepositions, Adverbs, and conjunctions. You can ask and answer questions and speak in Affirmation and Negation.

In this final section of the book, you will find some useful Vocabulary, some popular Colloquial words, and six more practical Conversations that you can use when visiting any Arab country. Using the following pages, you will be more comfortable conversing on common topics such as meeting and greeting, going places, staying in a hotel, and ordering at a restaurant.

Note: If you want to use the colloquial option in the Conversations:

1. *The words in Grey are the Colloquial version.*
2. *The letters in grey are:*

   - Unpronounced short vowels when the word lies at the end of speech.

   - Short vowels in the Classical word that can be omitted to transfer the Classical into Colloquial.

3. *Try to also apply the rules you learnt in transferring the Classical to Colloquial in the conversations and use as many words as possible from the Colloquial words list.*

You will also find the second stage of 'The Sentence Game' at the end of the book so that you can practice all your vocabulary and sentence forming in a very enjoyable way.

Remember that to master any language, you need to keep practicing. Don't forget to visit our website **www.knowarabic.co.uk** to check out the Audio files there and some more valuable information about Arabic.

Useful Vocabulary

Phonetics	English translation	الكَلِمَات
Atta7eyya	**Greetings**	**التَّحِيَّة**
Salam	Peace (also used for greeting)	سَلام
Assalamu-Alaikum	Greeting (literally: The peace be upon you)	السَّلامُ عَلَيْكُم
Marhaba	Hello	مَرْحَبا
Ahlan wa Sahlan	Hello	أَهْلًا وَ سَهْلًا
Sabah-el-Kheir	Good morning	صَباحِ الخير
Masa-el-kheir	Good evening	مَساءِ الخير
Ma-Assalama	Goodbye	مَعَ السَّلامَة
Words of Politeness	**Translation**	**كَلِماتُ الأَدَبْ**
Na'am	Yes	نَعَمْ
Laa	No	لا
Shukran	Thank you	شُكْرًا
Afwan / Al3afw	Welcome	عَفْوًا / العَفْو
Aasef Single **M**	Sorry	آسِف
Aasefa Single **F** Asfa		آسِفَة آسْفَه
Tafaddal Single **M** Et-faddal Tafaddali Single **F** Et-faddali Tafaddaloo **Plural** Et-faddaloo	Here you go/Please have/Please come in	تَفَضَّل اِتْفَضَّل تَفَضَّلي اِتْفَضَّلي تَفَضَّلوا اِتْفَضَّلوا
Lahza men fadlek	A moment please	لَحْظَة مِن فَضْلِك

Taqdeem-Annafs	Self-introduction	تَقْديمُ النَّفْس
Ana	I	أَنا
Ant**a** **M** Enta Ant**i** **F** Enti	You	أَنْتَ إِنْتَ أَنْتِ إِنْتِ
Esm	Name	إِسْم
Esmee	My name	إِسْمي
Esmok**a** **M** Esmak Esmok**i** **F** Esmek	Your name	إِسْمُكَ إِسْمَك إِسْمُكِ إِسْمِك
Ma Esmok**a**? **M** Esmak Eeh/Aesh? Ma Esmok**i**? **F** Esmek Eeh/Aesh?	What's your name?	ما إِسْمُكَ؟ إِسْمَكَ إيه/ إيش؟ ما إِسْمُكِ؟ إِسْمِكَ إيه/ إيش؟
Men Ayn**a**? Men Fein / Men Wein	From where	مِنْ أَيْنَ ؟ مِنْ فين / مِنْ وين؟
Sa'eed **M** – Sa'eedah **F** Be Moqabaletik	Glad to meet you	سَعيد – سَعيدة بِمُقابَلَتِك
Raqam Telephone	Phone number	رَقَم تليفون
Nathreyyat	**Miscellaneous**	نَثْرِيّات
Allughat-ul-3arabeyya	The Arabic language	اللُّغَةُ العَرَبِيَّة
3arabee	Arabic	عَرَبي
Ta3ala – Ta3alee – Ta3aloo	Come **M – F – Plural**	تَعالى – تَعالي – تَعالوا
Yaa	Oh! (Used for Calling someone)	يا

Aydan Kaman	Also – As well	أَيْضًا كَمان
Koll	All	كُلّ
Le-Anna	Because	لِأَنَّ
Laww	If	لَوْ
Bedoon	Without	بِدونْ
Faqat	Only	فَقَطْ
Awwalan	Firstly	أَوَّلًا
Akheeran	Finally	أَخيرًا

Note: Colloquial words are in grey.

Popular Colloquial Words

Phonetics	Translation	الكَلِمَات
Aywa/Ee	Yes	أَيْوَه / إي
La'	No	لأ
7adretak **M** 7adretek **F** 7adaratko **Plural**	You: - To formally address someone/people. - To show respect when speaking to an older person or someone of a higher rank.	حَضْرِتَك حَضْرِتِك حَضَراتْكو
7ader	OK (Word of politeness)	حاضِر
3ayez – Abee – Baddee **M** 3ayza – Abee – Baddee **F**	I want (Egyptian – Gulf – Levant)	عايِزْ – أَبي – بَدّي عايزَه – أَبي – بَدّي
Ezzayak – Eshlonak – keefak? **M** Ezzayek – Eshlonek – keefek? **F** Ezzayokom – Eshlonkom – keefkom? **Plural**	How are you? (Egyptian – Gulf – Levant)	إزَّيَّك – إشْلونَك – كيفَك؟ إزَّيِّك – إشْلونِك – كيفِك؟ إزَّيَّكُم – إشْلونْكُم – كيفْكُم؟
Mama Baba	Mother Father	ماما بابا
Sa7	Correct	صَحّ
Ghalat	Wrong	غَلَط
Mashi	OK	ماشي
Yalla	Come on	يالّا

Tayyeb	OK/Good	طَيِّب
Momken	Possible/Maybe	مُمْكِن
Moo – Mosh	Not	مِش – مو
Bass	Only/Stop! / That's it/But	بَسّ
Khalas	Finished/Done/Ok	خَلاصْ
Lessa	Not yet/Still	لِسَّه
Hat – Hati – Hato Khod – Khodi – khodo	Give me **M – F – Plural** Take **M – F – Plural**	هاتْ – هاتي – هاتو خُدْ – خُدي – خدو
Boss – Bossi – Bosso	Look **M – F – Plural**	بُصّ – بُصّي – بُصّو
Kaman	Also/More	كَمان
Kowayyes	Good	كُوَيِّس
Tamam	Perfect	تَمام
Lazem	Must	لازِم
Beddabt	Exactly	بِالضَّبْط
Berra7a	Gently	بِالرّاحَة
Shwayya	A bit/Little	شوَيَّة
Jeddan (Geddan) / Awee	Allot/Very	جِدًّا / أوي
7aja (7aga)	Something	حاجَة
Ya3nee	Meaning...	يَعْني
Da **M** – De **F**	This	دَه – دِه
Keda	Like this	كِده

Zayy	Like/Similar	زَيّ
Mathalan	For example	مَثَلًا
Ya3nee	Meaning/Sort of	يَعْني
Laww	If	لَوْ
Walla	Or	وَلّا
Kan	Was	كان
Ana Malee?	What concerns me? (It doesn't concern me)	أنا مالي
Ya Rate	I wish	يا ريت
Fee (ه is silent)	There is	فيه
Ma Feesh – Ma Fee	There isn't	ما فيش – ما فيه
Beta3ee – Malee – Eli Beta3tee – Malee – Eli Betoo3ee – Malooti – Eli	Mine referring to a **S**ingular **M**asculine Mine referring to a **S**ingular **F**eminine Mine referring to **P**lural (Egyptian – Gulf – Levant)	بِتاعي – مالي – إلي بِتاعْتي – مالْتي – إلي بِتوعي – مالوتي – إلي
Ba7ebbak – A7ebbak – B7ebbak Ba7ebbek – A7ebbek – B7ebbek Ba7ebbokom – A7ebkom – B7ebkom	I love you said to **M** I love you said to **F** I love you said to **P**lural (Egyptian – Gulf – Levant)	بَحِبَّك – أَحِبَّك – بْحِبَّك بَحِبِّك – أَحِبِّك – بْحِبِّك بَحِبُّكُم – أَحِبْكُم – بْحِبْكُم
7abeebi 7abebti 7abaybee	My beloved said to a **M**ale My beloved said to a **F**emale My beloved Said to a Group	حَبيبي حَبيبتي حَبايْبي

ح = 7   ع = 3

Conversation 1.

Meeting and greeting المُقابَلَة وَ التَّحِيَّة

Assalamu Alaikum

السَّلامُ عَلَيْكُم.

The peace be upon you

Walaikum Assalam

وَ عَلَيْكُمُ السَّلام.

And the peace be upon you

Kayf-al Haal

كَيْفَ الحال؟

How is the condition? (How are you / How is it going)

BeKhayr, AlHamdulellah

بِخَيْر، الحَمْدُ لِلَّه.

Well, Thanks to Allah (God). (Used often in Arab and Muslim Countries)

Ana Esmee .... Wa Anta/Wa antee ?

أَنا إِسْمي .... وَ أَنْتَ ؟ وَ أَنْتِ؟

My name is............. and you (M/F)?

Ana Esmee ....

أَنا إِسْمي ......

My name is ....

Conversation 2

Where are you from?   مِنْ أَيْنَ أَنْتَ ؟

First person:	Assalamu Alaikum	السَّلامُ عَلَيْكُم.
Second person:	Wa alaikum Assalam	وَ عَلَيْكُمُ السَّلام.

First person:	Kayf-Al-Haal ?	كَيْفَ الحال؟
Second person:	Bekhayr, Alhamdulellah	بِخَيْرٍ، الحَمْدُ لِلّه.

First person: Ana Esmee ……….   أَنا إِسْمي ………..

Wa Anta/Anti, Ma Esmoka/Esmoki ?   وَ أَنْتَ/ أَنْتِ ما إِسْمُكَ / إِسْمُكِ؟

Second person: Marhaba ………. Ana Esmee……….   مَرْحبا ………. أَنا إِسْمي……….

First person: Men Ayna Anta/Anti ya ……….?   مِنْ أَيْنَ أَنْتَ / أَنْتِ يا …….؟

Second person: Men Britania, Wa Anta/Anti?   مِنْ بريطانْيا وَ أَنْتَ / أَنْتِ ؟

First person: Ana men ……….   أَنا مِن ………..

Second person: Ana Sa'eed/Sa'eeda Bi Moqabaletik   أَنا سَعيد / سَعيدَة بِمُقابَلَتِك.

First person: Wa Ana Aydan   *Wana Kaman*   وَ أَنا أَيْضا. وَ انا كَمان

Conversation 3

Work العَمَل – المِهْنَة

1st Person:	Sabah-ElKheir.		صَباحِ الخير.

Morning of the goodness (Good Morning).

2nd Person: Sabah-Ennoor.   صَباحِ النّور.

Morning of the light (Good Morning-Reply).

1st Person: Kaifa Haloka ? *Kafe Halak*   M   كَيْفَ حالُكَ؟   كيف حالَك

Kaifa Haloki ? *Kafe Halek*   F   كَيْفَ حالُكِ؟   كيف حالِك

How are you doing?

2nd Person: Tamam, Wa Anta ? *Wenta*   M   تَمام. وَأَنْتَ؟ وِ انْتَ

Perfect (All good), and you?

Tamam, Wa Anti ? *Wenti*   F   تَمام. وَأَنْتِ؟ وِ انْتِ

Perfect (All good), and you?

1st Person: Kollo Tamam.   كُلُّه تَمام .

All is good.

أَنا إِسْمي .... مِنْ لَنْدَن وَ أَعْمَل أَشْتَغَل مُهَنْدِس / مُهَنْدِسَة.

Ana Esmee.......... Men London wa A3mal *Ashtaghal* Muhandes (M) / Muhandesa (F).

My name is.......... From London, and I work as an engineer.

2nd Person: أَهْلاً ....! وَ أَنا إِسْمي .... وَ أَعْمَل أَشْتَغَل مُدَرِّس/ مُدَرِّسَة.

Ahlan ....! Wa Ana *Wana* Esmee .... Wa A3mal *Ashtaghal*
Mudarress (M) / Mudarressa (F).

Hello ....! And my name is .... And I work as a teacher.

1st Person : Kaifa Haalo-Al3amal ? *Ashoghl*   كَيْفَ حالُ العَمَل؟ الشُّغْل

How is work going?

2nd Person : Jayyed , Laken Mut3eb Qaleelan.   جَيِّد، لكِن مُتْعِب قَليلًا .

Kuwayyes Bass mot3eb Showayya /Shwayy.   كُوَيِّس، بَسّ مُتْعِب شُوَيَّة/شوَيّ.

Good, but a little tiring.

Conversation 4

From the Airport to the Hotel   مِنَ المَطارِ إلى الفُنْدُق

<u>Outside the Airport</u>

خَارِجُ المَطار

- السّائِقِ السَّوَاق: صَباحِ الخير.

Driver: Good Morning (*literally Morning of goodness*).

Assa'eq: Saba7-el Kheir.

- السّائِح: صَباحِ النّور.

Tourist: Good Morning (*literally Morning of light*).

Assae'7: Sabe7-Ennoor.

- السّائِقِ: تاكْسي؟

Driver: Taxi?

Assa'eq: Taxi?

- السّائِح: نَعَم . تَعْرِفُ فُنْدُقَ النَّجْمَة؟

Tourist: Yes. You know The Star Hotel?

Assae'7: Na3am, Ta3refo Fondoq-Annajma?

- السّائِق: نَعَم أَعْرِف الفُنْدُق، تَفَضَّل.

Driver: Yes, I know the hotel, come in (in polite expression).

Assae'q: Na3am, A3ref-AlFondoq, Tafaddal.

- السّائِح: كَم الأُجْرَة؟

Tourist: How much is the fair?

Assae'7:   Kam-el-Ujrah?

- السّائِق: عَلى حَسَب العَدّاد. تمام؟

Driver: According to the Meter. That's fine?

Assa'eq: 3ala 7asab- Al3addad. Tamam?

- السّائِح: تَمام.

Tourist: That's fine/Prefect.

Assa'e7:   Tamam.

Conversation 5

At the hotel في الفُنْدُق

- مُوَظَّفَةُ الاسْتِقْبال: مَرْحَبا !

Receptionist: Hello !

Mowazzafat-AlEsteqbal: Mar7aba !

- السّائِح: مَرْحَبا ! مِنْ فَضْلِك عِنْدي حَجْز بِإِسْم ....

Tourist: Hello. Please, I have a reservation by the name.....

Assa'e7:   Mar7aba. Men Fadlek 3endee 7ajz be-Esm.....

- مُوَظَّفَةُ الاسْتِقْبال: لَحْظَة مِنْ فَضْلِك. نَعَم، الحَجْز مَوْجُود. مُمْكِن الباسْبور (جَوازُ السَّفَر) ؟

Receptionist: A moment please. Yes, the reservation is there *(literally: exists).* Can I have the passport?

Mowazzafat-AlEsteqbal: La7tha Men Fadlek. Na3am, Al 7ajz Mawjood. Momken-AlPasspore (Jawaz-Assafar)?

- السّائِح: نَعَم، تَفَضَّلي.

Tourist: Yes, here you go.

Assae'7: Na3am Tafaddalee.

- مُوَظَّفَةُ الاسْتِقْبال: شُكْرًا. الغُرْفَة جاهِزَة . تَفَضَّل المُفْتاح.

Receptionist: Thank you. The room is ready. Here is the key.

Mowazzafat-AlEsteqbal: Shukran. Al-Ghorfa Jaheza. Tafaddal-Al Mofta7.

- السّائِح: مُمْتاز . أَيْن وين المَطْعَم؟

Tourist: Excellent. Where is the restaurant?

Assae'7: Momtaz. Ayna Wane Almat3am?

- مُوَظَّفَةُ الاسْتِقْبال: المَطْعَم في الطّابِق الأَرْضي. إقامَة سَعيدَة !

Receptionist: The restaurant is on the Ground Floor. Have a nice stay!

Mowazzafat-AlEsteqbal: Al-Mat3am fe-Ttabeq-Al Ardee. Iqama Sa3eida.

- السّائِح: شُكْرًا. مَع السَّلامَة.

Tourist: Thank you. Goodbye.

Assae'7: Shukran ma3a-Assalama.

Conversation 6

Visiting places زِيارَةُ الأَماكِن

- السّائِح: صباحِ الخير.

The Tourist: Good Morning (Literally: morning of goodness).

Assa'e7:   Saba7-ElKheir.

- مُوَظَّف خِدْمَةُ العُمَّلاء: صَباحِ النّور.

Guest Relations Employee: Good morning *(literally Morning of light)*.

Mowathaf Khedmat-Al3omala': Saba7-Ennoor.

- السّائِح: مِنْ فَضْلِك ما هِيَ (إيه – إيش – شو) الأَماكِن السِّياحِيَّة القَريبَة مِنَ الفُنْدُق؟

The Tourist: Please, what are the touristic places near to the Hotel?

Assa'e7: Men Fadlek, Ma heya (Eih-Aesh-Shoo) Al-Amaken-Asseya7eyya-AlQareebah men-Al Fondoq?

- المُوَظَّف: الأَماكِن القَريبة هِي المَتْحَف الوَطَني وَ مَرْكَز التَّسَوُّق المول.

The Employee: The near places are the National Museum and the Mall.

Al-Mowazzaf: Al-Amaken-AlQareeba heya-AlMat7af-AlWatanee wa Markaz-Attasawwoq
Al-Mall.

- السَّائِح: تَمام. تَعْرِفُ مَواعيد الزِّيارَة لِلْمَتْحَف؟

The Tourist: Perfect. Do you know the visiting times for the Museum?

Assa'e7:   Tamam. Ta3refo mawa3eed-Azzeyara lelMat7af?

- المُوَظَّف: نَعَم أَيْوَه. مِنَ السّاعَة التّاسِعَة تِسْعَه صَباحًا إلى السّاعَة الخامِسَة خَمْسَه مَساءً.

The Employee: Yes. From Nine AM to Five PM.

AlMowathaf: Na3am Aywah. Men-Assa3a-Attase3a Tes3ah Saba7an Ela-Assa3a-AlKhamesa Khamsa Masa'an.

- السّائِح: طَيِّب، شُكْرًا. مُمْكِن تَطْلُب لي تاكْسي؟

The Tourist: Ok, Thank you. Can you order a taxi for me?

Assa'e7:   Tayyeb Shokran. Momken tatlob-lee Taxi?

- المْوَظَّف: نَعَم طَبْعا. التّاكْسي سَيَصِل بَعْدَ عَشَر دَقائِق.

Employee: Yes of course. The Taxi will arrive after 10 minutes.

AlMowathaf: Na3am Tab3an. Attaxi sayaselo ba3da 3ashar daqa'eq.

- السّائِح: شُكْرًا.

The Tourist: Thank you.

Assa'e7:   Shokran.

- المُوَظَّف: عَفْوًا.

The Employee: You are welcome.

AlMowathaf: 3afwan.

Congratulations!   مَبْروك

You have reached the end of the Book! And I hope you enjoyed your journey. You are now ready to use all that you learned to read, write, and speak well in Arabic. Now enjoy all the knowledge you have learned and keep practicing.

As you know from Part 1, we have designed a special Game for you to help you remember all the words that you learned in Part 2, and to practice forming sentences in a fun way: **The Sentence Game**. You can play using Part 2 words only, or all the words in Part 1 and Part 2 tables. All you need to do is to cut the words off the tables to form a playing Deck, and you can also laminate it yourself if you like. You will enjoy this game individually, and you will enjoy it even more in a group of 2 or more.

Enjoy the Game!

بالتَّوْفيق

The Sentence Game Instructions

Game Objective

The objective for each player is to use all their cards by forming sentences with a minimum of two cards per sentence. The first player to finish their cards wins the game.

Assembling The Sentence Game

Distribute the cards so that each player receives 14 cards, then place the remaining cards nearby, as this will be used during the game as a draw pile.

Rules

1. Every player, at the beginning of each turn, draws a word from the pile of cards. Then he tries to form as many sentences as possible with his cards and puts them down. If a player is unable to form any sentence with the drawn card, they pass.

2. If you have a blank card, you may use this in the place of any other word to form your sentence.

3. A player can use their turn to adapt previously formed sentences made by any other player. They can do this by:

• Adding one or more cards to the beginning, middle, or end of a sentence (as long as the produced sentence makes sense).

• Swapping out one word with another, then using the swapped card in a sentence of its own. Swapped cards must be used in the same turn.

• A player can also use the swapping method if the word they are swapping is a blank card, in which case they can change it to become a new word.

4. Once a player uses all their cards, the Game is over. Collect all the cards used in sentences and set them aside in a separate pile. You can then use the remaining card-drawing pile to begin a new game with different words.

5. Repeat this process until you have used all the words, then shuffle and start again.

The winner can now 'sentence' the losers with the verdict of their choosing ;)

Enjoy!

إِبْن	أَتَكَلَّم	اِجْلِس
أُحِبّ	اِدْخُل	أَرْبَعَةَ عَشَر
أُريد	إِسْم	إِسْمُك
اِسْمَعوا	أَعْمَل	ال
ال	الآن	إِلّا
الّتي	الّذان	الّذي
الّذين	إلى	أَلْف
اِمْسَحي	أَنْتَ	أَنْتِ
أَنْ	أَنْتُم	أَيّ

بَعْد	بِ	أَيْنَ
بَيْض	بَنات	بِكَم
تُحِبّ	تَتَكَلَّم	تَأْكُل
تُريدين	تُريدون	تُريد
تَفَضَّل	تَعْمَل	تَعَلَّم
تَقْريبًا	تَقْرَأ	تَفَضَّلي
تَفْهَمين	تَشْرَب	تَسْمَع
ثُلْث	الثّانِيَة	تَمامًا
جِدًّا	ثَمانين	ثُمَّ

حَضَرْنا	حَتّى	حَتّى
دَجاج	خَمْسَة وَ ثَلاثون	خُبْز
الدَّوْلي	دَقيقَة	دَرْس
رِجال	رُبْع	ذَهَبَ
سَأَخْرُج	زائِر	رَقَم
ساعَة	السّادِسَة	سَ
سَيَفْتَح	سَمَك	السّاعَة
صَباحًا	شِمال	شُكْرًا
صوت	صَديق	صَباح الخير

عام	العاشِرَة	الصّورَة
عَصير	عَسَل	العَرْض
عُمّال	عَلى	عَفْوًا
غَيْر	عِنْدَ	عَنْ
قِطّتان	فَوْقَ	قَبْلَ
كَ	كَ	قَهْوَة
كُما	كُمْ	كَمْ
لا	لِ	كَيْفَ
اللُّغَةُ العَرَبِيّة	لَحْظة	لا

لِماذا	لَنْ	لَيْسَ
ما	مائَة	ماذا
متى	مُحِبّ	المَحَلّ
مُدَرِّسات	مَرْحَبا	مَساءً
مساء الخير	المَسْرَح	مِنْ فَضْلك
المَطار	مَطْعَم	مُغَنّي
مُمْكِن	مَنْ	مُهَنْدِس
نَحْنُ	نَفْتَح	نَعَم
ه	ها	هَلْ

هُناك	هُنا	هُم
هِيَ	هُوَ	هُنَّ
واحِد	و	و
ي	ي	واحِدة
يَشْرَبون	يَتَكَلَّمْنَ	نا
يَعْمَلْنَ	يَعْمَل	يَتَعَلَّم
		يَمين